1446
PHOTO
TIPS

1446 PHOTO TIPS

Harmony Books/New York

Conceived, edited and designed by
Duncan Associates,
64 Fullerton Road, London SW18 1BX
with Mel Petersen & Associates
5 Botts Mews, Chepstow Road
London W2 5AG

Published by Harmony Books, a division
of Crown Publishers, Inc., 225, Park Avenue South,
New York, New York 10003.

HARMONY and colophon are trademarks of
Crown Publishers, Inc.

Manufactured in Great Britain.

Tips compiled by John Farndon, Michael
Freeman, John Heseltine, David Hoffman, Gene
Nocon, Richard Platt, Nick Scott and Tim
Shackleton.

Assignments written by John Farndon in
collaboration with Cliff Feulner, David Hamilton,
Monique Fay, Heather Angel, Stephen Dalton,
Eamonn McCabe, Bill and Claire Leimbach,
James Barrow, Brian Griffin, Paddy Eckersley,
Chris Alan Wilton, Helena Zakrzewska-Rucinska,
Liz Hollingworth, Michael Freeman, Anthea
Sieveking and Roy Flooks.

Special consultants: Peter Samwell and staff of
Fujimex, UK distributors of Fuji film and cameras.

Library of Congress Cataloging in Publication Data
Main entry under title:

1446 Photo Tips.

    Includes index.
    1. Photography—Handbooks, manuals, etc.
I. Title.   II. Title: 1446 Photo Tips.
TR146.A12   1984   770   83-22591
ISBN 0-517-55316-3

10 9 8 7 6 5 4 3 2

First Edition

MAKING THE MOST OF PHOTO TIPS

1446 Photo Tips is intended to be as useful for browsing in as for looking up specific problems.

The cross-references

Each numbered tip makes sense read in isolation, but those with a minimal knowledge of photography will meet a few terms and concepts they do not understand. As far as possible, such terms and concepts are supplied with a cross-reference to a tip (or tips) elsewhere in the book which explains or defines. If there is no such cross-reference, look up the term or concept in the contents section.

Some of the tips need to be read either in sequence or in relation to other tips to gain the fullest picture. Important sequences are introduced by a tip with a headline followed by tips with numbers only. Related tips are indicated by cross-references: *see* followed by a tip number indicates an essential cross-reference; *see also* and a tip number indicates an optional cross-reference.

Sequence of tips

Open the book at any page, and you will find the tips arranged in sequence. Generally, a sequence covering a single area runs across a double-page spread, beginning at the top of the first broad-measure column of the left-hand page. Basic reminders generally come first, followed by tips on increasingly complex or advanced considerations, ending at the foot of the right-hand page.

Sometimes a single area is covered on one page; sometimes over several spreads.

The outer, boxed columns

The two text columns at the extreme left- and right-hand sides of every spread, headed with an exclamation mark, carry cautions: warnings needing special emphasis. Always read them with the rest of the tips on the spread or page.

The six sections

1446 Photo Tips is in six sections: **Technique** covering basic skills and explaining basic concepts; **Subjects,** about tailoring one's approach to individual subjects; **Assignments,** translating these first two sections into the reality of colour pictures. **Equipment,** about assessing one's needs and buying wisely, works hand-in-hand with the opening spreads of **Technique. Processing and Darkroom** and **Storage and Presentation** are self-explanatory.

The contents section

If you need a quick answer to a photographic problem, or want to explore a specific area, use the contents section. It lists every tip, and every sequence of tips, along with summaries of what the tips cover. Cautions are generally listed by number only – they should be read anyway. Especially important cautions are indicated by a short summary. Occasionally, 'regular' tips come into the category of essential reading, and are listed in the contents section as cautions.

Photography's various fields are closely interrelated, so don't just look up your problem or area of interest in one section. This is especially true of tips in **Technique,** which are likely to have counterparts under **Subjects** and **Equipment.**

1

CONTENTS

TECHNIQUE

SECTION

CONTENTS

SUBJECTS SECTION

4

7

CONTENTS

ASSIGNMENTS

SECTION

CONTENTS

EQUIPMENT

SECTION

TECHNIQUE

Basic photographic skills • The camera, and film for the job
Handling a camera • Using the controls • Understanding light
Flash • Using accessories • Being prepared

1
Think before you take an SLR on a holiday by the sea – they are particularly prone to damage by salt and sand. If you simply want snapshots of holiday scenes, a cheap compact is less of a worry.

2
Don't forget that all SLRS (except autofocus models) must be properly focused for each shot. For casual, off-the-cuff candids – at a party, for instance – use a simpler camera.

3
Beware of the loud clack of the mirror as you take a picture with an SLR – it may disturb your subject. When stealth is crucial – in wildlife photography and candid portraits, for instance – an SLR may be unsuitable.

4 The 35mm SLR
If you want the most versatile camera possible, there is really only one choice: the 35mm single lens reflex camera or SLR. You can take equally impressive pictures on other types of camera, but only with an SLR can you shoot so effectively in so many conditions.

5 Reflex viewing
For the critical attention to composition and focusing demanded by quality photography, an SLR is ideal. The SLR viewing system shows you the scene through the lens exactly as the film 'sees' it. Only costly professional cameras can rival the SLR in this respect – and even they cannot beat an SLR for easy close-ups.

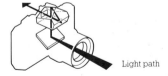

Light path

6 Changing lenses
For many types of photograph, such as wildlife, sports and even portraits, the standard lens on a camera is less than ideal. With an SLR, you can fit different lenses to give the best effect with an excitingly wide range of subjects.

7 System building
A 35mm SLR is the camera to use if you see photography as a permanent, widening interest and you want a camera for both high-quality pictures and specialist applications. The range of accessories in 35mm SLR systems is vast – whatever your special interest, the right accessory is usually there – from microscope attachments to 'shift' lenses for architectural photography.

8 TTL metering
When you fit filters and other attachments to the front of a lens, exposure is affected. If you use an SLR, you are spared the need to calculate compensation because its through the lens (TTL) metering system measures the light actually falling on the film. Not only this, but as the manufacturers claim, TTL metering is an extremely convenient, fast way of determining exposure.

9 Automation?
If you are a complete beginner, you may be tempted to the simplicity and ease of operation of SLRS with fully automated exposure systems. But their very simplicity may be a drawback: because exposure is taken out of your hands, you may never develop a 'feel' for it. So a manual might be a better bet for a first SLR.

10 Action shots
To freeze fast action properly, you need a fast shutter speed. An SLR, with its focal plane shutter, gives the widest range of shutter speeds of any camera type outside the field of specialist equipment.

Disc camera

Pocket camera

11 Pocket cameras

Simple cameras using cartridge or disc film are ideal for snapshots. They're cheap, easy to load and have few (if any) controls to fuss over.

12 Quality

Pocket cameras cannot give the quality of 35mm models, nor are they as versatile – some can only be used on sunny days or with flash. But providing you recognize their limitations, and take care over composition, you can take perfectly satisfactory pictures. Go for complex equipment only if you think you can master it.

13 Awkward hands

The pocket camera, with its slot-in film and big, easy-to-press shutter button, is perfect for children or for adults who find most cameras too fiddly to operate. Those with automatic flash and film wind-on are even more trouble-free, letting you devote your attention exclusively to getting an interesting shot of your subject.

14 Film choice

Remember that most of the film made for pocket cameras is for colour prints. You may have problems obtaining colour slide or black and white materials. If you feel you'd like to break out of the 'family album' format a 35mm camera would be a better choice.

15 Holiday snaps

If you want a carefree camera for snaps on the beach, a walk in the park or a family outing, a cartridge or disc camera is the one to use. Most are plastic, but their neat, simple design means they stand up well to wear and tear. Some are designed to be weatherproof, a boon if you spend a lot of your leisure time outdoors (skiing or sailing perhaps) and could use the extra protection.

16 Visual notebook

Even serious photographers shouldn't turn their noses up at a pocket camera. They can be used for quick reference shots without hassles.

17 Versatility

You can shoot in a wide variety of conditions with an automatic pocket camera while one with a slide-in telephoto lens increases your versatility. But these facilities cost money – a 35mm camera with the same capabilities may be as cheap.

18 Moving subjects

Action pictures are restricted with a pocket camera. Shutters are usually fixed at 1/60 (cartridge) or 1/100 (disc). Any movement above walking pace may come out blurred.

19
Don't use a pocket or disc camera if you want to blow up the pictures bigger than postcard size – the quality could be disappointing.

20
Don't use a pocket camera if you want many copies of a single shot – the negatives can be bleached out by the intense light used for printing.

21
Beware of covering the lens with a finger when taking a picture. The viewfinder of a pocket camera is set to one side and you can easily fail to spot a stray digit in the way.

THE CAMERA FOR THE JOB

22
Don't forget that you can override an all-automatic camera's exposure meter by adjusting the film speed dial (see **157**) to give more or less exposure as required, thus increasing the creative potential.

23
Don't be misled by the sharpness of a viewfinder image. Unless there is an autofocus mechanism, the lens must be focused for every shot. Unlike an SLR, the compact does not allow you to see how accurately you have focused.

Canon AF35M

24 The 35mm compacts
If you want 35mm quality, and the opportunity to use a wide range of film types, consider a compact camera as an alternative to the more complex 35mm SLR. They are lighter – and by being mostly automatic – far easier to use.

25 For beginners
Compacts make good first cameras. You can learn the basics of photography without getting obsessed with exposure and focusing (they're taken care of by the automatic functions) and you won't be embarrassed by the quality of the results.

26 For the SLR owner
Many professionals and serious amateurs own a compact camera as well as an SLR. The latter – if used with a range of interchangeable lenses and other accessories – can be too bulky to carry around all the time. But a compact with a good lens can be tucked into a pocket and forgotten about until a picture opportunity suddenly presents itself.

27 Candid shots
For off-the-cuff shots, when you have no time to set exposure and focus controls, an auto-matic compact is ideal. The wide-angle lens gives greater coverage than an SLR's standard lens, and the automatic focus is fast and accurate. But see **43** for situations where the focusing sensor can be misled.

28 Quiet shutter
The almost silent operation of the compact camera's leaf shutter can be a great help if you do not want to attract attention to yourself. This may be very important if you want to take a lot of candid or wildlife pictures.

29 Shutter speeds
Though you might feel restricted by a compact camera's limited range of shutter speeds (for most cameras this is between 1/30 and 1/500) compared with an SLR, most SLR owners will tell you that they use speeds beyond this range only rarely.

30 Film advance
The automated film advance fitted to some compacts is certainly an operating convenience if you're in a hurry. But since it only advances a single frame at a time (unlike a motor drive, where you have the facility for continuous operation) you can't really take the kind of action sequences that some manufacturers' advertising suggests is possible with such cameras.

31 Close-ups
Take care when framing close-ups with a compact. Use the special framing marks in the viewfinder to align the subject correctly (see **210–211**).

Kodak EK160   Polaroid 30

32 Instant picture

With an instant picture camera, you get immediate results – a finished print seconds after taking the picture. But before you fall for the obvious attractions of such a camera, decide just how important the instant result is to you. There are drawbacks instant prints are generally small and cannot be enlarged; making duplicates is not as straightforward as with conventional film and prints can lose their colour faster than conventional ones.

33 Fun photography

If you want photography to be fun, you cannot do better than an instant picture camera. Although features vary from model to model all are simple to use and are ideal for shots around the house, at parties and out with friends. You can snap people in amusing situations and show them the results instantly for a spot reaction.

34 The right film

You lose some of the advantages of instant picures if you use a camera that takes the older 'peel apart' film rather than the newer 'integral' film.

Peel apart prints are rather messy for handing around after the picture is taken. Also, the covering cannot be removed until processing is complete – so you miss out on the magic of seeing the picture appear.

35 Simple or complex

Some instant picure cameras have sophisticated autofocus and autoexposure systems. If you mostly use a camera for 'at home' shots, all you need is a basic model. And it is worth bearing in mind that the simplest instant picture cameras are very cheap.

36 Bulk

While instant picture cameras are good to have around the house for casual shots, they are maddeningly bulky to carry out of doors. Some SLR Polaroids fold flat, however

Polaroid SX70

37 Instant trial shots

One of the most useful ways of employing an instant picture camera is for trial shots to discover whether or not a photo to be taken on a conventional camera actually works. This is especially valuable with still lifes – you can see instantly if the light falls badly, if the shot is well composed and if there are ugly distractions.

38
Never cut, scratch or crease a print made on integral material. This can cause irreparable damage. Fingerprints can be removed by breathing gently on the affected areas and wiping the marks with a soft cloth or tissue.

39
Don't forget that you cannot use Kodak film in a Polaroid instant picture camera, and vice versa. Colour rendition varies between film brands, too. So if you are buying a new instant picture camera, find out which results you like best and let that be a factor in deciding which model to buy.

40
Don't waste costly instant picture film by making persistent exposure errors. Learn to recognize the situations where you've had to use the lighten/darken control to correct a too-dark or too-light first attempt. In future, anticipate these and use the control right from the start – before shooting.

41 Exposure
Almost all instant picture cameras have automatic exposure – reliable in many situations but capable of being misled by certain subjects (see **152 – 155**). Use the lighten/darken control to allow more or less exposure to compensate for such errors, as well as to correct initially over- or underexposed shots.

42 Close-ups
You can come in closer than an instant picture camera's minimum given focusing distance, but only if you use a close-up attachment (which may however be built into some models).

43 Autofocus
Automatic focusing devices can usually be relied on if, in the case of infrared and ultrasonic systems, the subject is centred in the picture or, for a contrast-comparing system, if it stands out moderately well from its surroundings. But in the picture below this has led the camera to focus on the fence. The image would have been more pleasing had the photographer intervened and focused (either manually or by using the memory lock) on the flowers to one side.

TLR – Mamiya C330

Rollfilm SLR – Hasselblad

44 Rollfilm cameras
With these cameras, a high premium is placed on the photographer's skills. Only very few, for instance, have built-in metering – a feature taken for granted with other cameras. You need a thorough grasp of the camera's exposure and focusing controls to take successful pictures.

45 Twin-lens reflex (TLR)
These cameras are designed so that normally you hold the camera at waist level and look down into the viewfinder. This is a great advantage when you are photographing people because you can maintain eye contact with them. On the other hand, taking action shots can be tricky – especially since the viewfinder image is laterally reversed. Most cameras allow you to view the subject directly at eye level through a simple 'sportsfinder' – an aperture in the focusing screen hood. The shutter is exceptionally quiet but few models accept interchangeable lenses. As these must be bought in pairs – the TLR system uses one lens for viewing and another for 'taking' – they are costly.

46 Rollfilm SLRs

To take full advantage of the rollfilm SLR's potential, you'll need to buy equipment costing two or three times as much as any 35mm equivalent. However, the particular features that attract professional fashion and portrait photographers especially to the rollfilm SLR are: superb definition; waist-level finder (which can be changed to an eye-level one having built-in metering); interchangeable film backs, allowing you to change from one type of film to another in midshoot. The range of interchangeable lenses is not as extensive as 35mm SLR systems'.

47 Film

As you can see below, rollfilm is four times the size of a 35mm negative. The advantage of the larger format is that big enlargements are sharper, have better contrast and are less grainy than those from smaller film sizes (likewise slides are crisper). The less the image has to be blown up, the more the original quality is retained. Against this you have to balance proportionally higher film costs. You would have to make a considerable number of exhibition-size prints to justify paying extra for film and the equipment to do justice to rollfilm's capabilities.

48
Don't make the high capital investment in a quality rollfilm system without deciding whether the benefits are worth the extra cost over 35mm. Are you taking the kind of pictures where pin-sharp image quality is all-important? Do you regularly make big enlargements? Will you be able to sell more transparencies and prints for reproduction? Can you take the time to deliberate over each shot, rather than relying on the speed and efficiency of automatic controls? Will you be happy with a limited amount of equipment? You can buy more for less with the 35mm format.

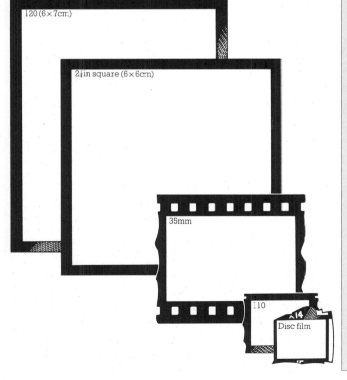

120 (6 × 7cm)

2¼in square (6 × 6cm)

35mm

110

Disc film

49
Don't let film lie around in a warm place, such as near a radiator or on the rear shelf of a car. Emulsion can be affected by heat.

50
Don't try out a new or unfamiliar type of film when you are photographing a rare or unrepeatable event. Its characteristics may be different to your usual brand, and you could find the results disappointing.

51
Don't forget to alter the film speed dial on your camera when changing to a film with a different speed rating. If you shoot off colour transparency film at the wrong setting, make sure you tell the processor what you have done – it may be possible to adjust processing and still produce acceptable results. Processors will generally not wish to compensate for exposure errors when developing negative film, but can do so (with some loss of image quality) when making prints.

52 Colour film types
Use colour negative film if you want to have prints made from your photographs. Prints are easy to pass around and display; extra copies are cheap.

53
Use reversal film if you want colour slides (transparencies). You will need either a hand viewer or a projector, but the result tends to be more realistic – definition is sharper and colours are brighter. Duplicate slides cost more than extra prints.

54
You can have prints made from slides, and slides made from prints, but the results are rarely as good as the original. Colours tend to be weaker, and contrast is emphasized.

55 B/w from colour
Black and white prints can be made from colour originals, but expect poorer quality.

56 Choosing colour film
Try different slide films until you find one whose colour rendition suits your taste. Some people, for instance, prefer the warm tone of Agfa film, and others think skin tones are more natural on Kodachrome. Fuji films respond well to green, Ektachrome to blue.

57 Stay with it
Having decided which brand of slide film you like, stick to it. The differences in colour reproduction between brands is very apparent when you see them together in a slide show.

58 Best match
For consistency, have all your prints made by the same lab. Brand differences with negative film are much less evident than with slides (though this is not the case with high-resolution films), but the actual prints may vary enormously depending on where they are produced.

59 'Free' film
The free colour print film offered as part of a processing deal may simply be what the company has in stock – often you can have no idea of what brand it will be. Treat such offers with suspicion unless you can be sure of exactly what you're getting.

60 Get the size right
Make sure you buy film in the right format for your camera: 110 or 126 cartridge film; disc film; 35mm cassettes; 120 or 127 rollfilm; instant picture packs. Remember that many films are made only in a small range of formats.

61 Film and light
Bear in mind that the speed of your film (a numerical rating of its sensitivity to light) to some extent dictates the apertures and shutter speeds you can use, and thus the kind of shots you can take.

62 Thinking ahead
Try to anticipate the lighting conditions you will encounter, and choose film accordingly. Whatever the weather forecast says, always pack a fast film in case conditions deteriorate.

63 Slow colour film

Use a film rated below 100 ISO if you want to capture fine detail with the minimum of grain. Generally speaking, the light will have to be pretty bright if you want to use fast shutter speeds to take action shots with this type of film.

64 Fast colour film

Use film rated at 400 ISO or higher for poor or unpredictable light. Being much more sensitive to light than slower films, this type allows you to shoot action pictures in all but the worst light. Slight miscalculations of exposure are less critical than with slow film, but the graininess of most fast films becomes apparent when you make sizeable enlargements – though not with high-resolution print film.

65 Medium-speed colour

Use a medium-speed film (rated between 100 and 200 ISO) if you are going to encounter various lighting conditions as you work your way through the film. But if you usually only have enprints made, there is little to be gained in terms of colour rendition and sharpness from using medium-speed conventional film in preference to a faster, high-resolution print film.

66 Light source

You must match slide film to the prevailing light source. Use daylight-type film when shooting in natural light or with flash. Use tungsten film for artificial light. Daylight film can be used in tungsten light, and tungsten film in daylight, only if you use certain filters. See **357, 359.**

67 Colour casts

You can shoot negative film in most light (except fluorescent) without conversion filters. The slight colour cast thus caused may add mood. Heavy casts can be removed during printing, if you ask for it. But it can't be done for prints made or an automatic machine. See **367.**

68 Storage

Keep your film in a cool, dry place away from any direct heat source. Some types of film designed for professional use must be kept chilled. Always consult the instructions.

69 Exposed films

Mark these with a coloured sticker once you have taken them out of the camera, or bend back the film leader. This will warn you against accidental reloading.

70 Processing

Have colour film processed as soon as possible. If you leave it longer than a month, the dyes may fade.

71

Check whether the price of the film includes processing by the manufacturer. If not, a camera shop or processing firm will do the job for you.

72

Most major towns and cities have labs processing E6 film (1216) to professional standards. Some offer mail-order service. Ask a professional to recommend such a lab to you, rather than rely on magazine advertisements.

73

Don't be afraid to complain to the processor about poor prints when they are plainly not your fault. Any reputable firm will make new prints for you at no extra charge, but see 1027.

74

Don't – unless you have seen good results from them – be tempted by firms offering processing and materials at rock-bottom prices. Quality control may be non-existent.

75

Don't put exposed film back in your bag along with your unexposed rolls. It's easy to reload an exposed film by accident, especially if – with 35mm film – the leader is still protruding from the cassette.

76

In case you forget what film you are using, tear off the end of the carton and slot it into the holder on the camera back – or tape it in a convenient place. See also 396.

77
Don't forget to have a spare fast film with you at all times – it will give you extra versatility should the light worsen.

78
Don't fully rewind cassette film if you do your own processing. You will find loading the film on to the spool easier if, when rewinding the film in the camera, you crank it back until the instant you feel the tension slacken off. This signifies that the exposed film has been wound back into the cassette but the leader is still protruding, thus saving you the trouble of prising the cassette open in the dark to get at the leader.

79
Don't soldier on with a slow film if the lighting gets worse. Wind it back until just the leader is protruding and on this mark the number of shots you have already taken. Reload it later when conditions improve, making blank exposures with the lens cap on to get back to the point at which you changed films.

80 Black and white film
Just as with colour film, take account of your subject and the lighting when deciding what film to use.

81
Slow film (50 ISO or less) has extremely fine grain, which makes it ideal for recording maximum detail and making big enlargements. Being less contrasty than faster films, it is useful in bright light.

82
Medium-speed film (125 ISO) needs reasonably bright light to bring out its best characteristics, but its grain and good definition make it an ideal general-purpose film.

83
Use a fast film (400 ISO) if you are likely to encounter a wide range of lighting, or if you want to use fast shutter speeds for action shots. Some photographers use this type of film exclusively in winter, switching to a slower film for the brighter summer months.

84 Chromogenic film
For a very fast ISO rating, or to obtain greatest latitude, use chromogenic film. It can be exposed at any setting from 1600 ISO down to (depending on brand) 400 or even 125 ISO. There is little visible variation in the overall result, except perhaps at the extremes of the range. You can shoot off part of the film at one setting and then change to a faster or slower rating. Grain and contrast are surprisingly acceptable at all speeds. See **930**.

85 Instant picture film
Black and white instant picture film comes in various formats and film speeds, right up to 3000 ISO. Grain is unnoticeable. Some types produce a reclaimable negative from which you can enlarge.

86 B/w transparencies
If you want to make black and white slides for projection, use either the proprietary film made specifically for this, or have conventional negative film reversal-processed. Slow film is best for the latter – give 1½ stops extra exposure.

87 Processing
You can process conventional black and white film easily at home. This will give you maximum control over contrast and grain in the negatives. (Chromogenic film – see **84** – needs C41 processing. Kits are available.)

88 Bulk film
Save money on black and white 35mm film by buying it in bulk and loading special, reloadable cassettes by means of a bulk loading device. Don't use conventional cassettes for this purpose, except in emergencies – they may not be lightproof and can accumulate dust and tiny grit particles which scratch the film.

89 Expiry dates
Just because a black and white film is past the 'process by' date on the pack it needn't be unusable. If it's been kept cool, it should be good for six more months. But use fresh stock for important work.

90 Changing ISO ratings

You can shoot black and white negatives and colour slides (but preferably not Kodachrome or colour negative film) at a different speed rating to that recommended by the maker, but you must adjust the development accordingly. For convenience, adjust exposure in whole or half stops.

91 Uprating film

If your film is too slow for the prevailing conditions (perhaps the light has become too dull, for instance) you can make it more sensitive by uprating its given ISO setting. You can shoot 200 ISO film at 400 or even 800 ISO, for example. But – unless you are using chromogenic film (see 84) – you must shoot the whole film at the revised setting. If you decide to uprate part-way through the film, the earlier shots will be overexposed. See next tip.

92 Pushing film

To compensate for having uprated the film, you must give increased development, so that a stronger image is produced. Normally you would increase the development time by 30% if you have doubled the rating, and by 80% if you have given a fourfold increase. Speed-enhancing developers giving a 2–3 stop increase are available for black and white film. Some photographers always overdevelop black and white film, even if it has been shot at the normal rating, as a way of giving extra contrast and shadow detail. This has little adverse effect, and is a useful way of ensuring that there is a sound basic negative.

93 Effects of pushing

If you push slide film by two stops or more, distortions in colour rendition will become apparent. Pushing enhances grain and contrast, so that shadows start to fill in and highlights appear harsher. It's better to shoot uprated film in flat, even lighting – bright, contrasty light will be uncomfortably emphasized.

94 Downrating film

If your camera is loaded with fast film but your subject is very contrasty – or too brilliantly lit – the results may show a 'soot and chalk' effect. Downrating the film to lower than its stated speed will lower contrast. Again, you must shoot off the whole film at the new, lower rating, unless you can sacrifice the shots you have already taken – they will turn out overexposed.

95 Pulling film

Give downrated film reduced development – this is known as 'pulling'. If you have halved the ISO rating, give 30% less development time. Reduce the development by 50% for film exposed at a quarter of its normal rating. The exact compensations needed when pushing and pulling vary according to the chemicals used – consult the instruction sheet.

96 Effects of pulling

Image contrast is reduced, so it is not a good idea to pull your film if the lighting is flat and the subject lacks contrast. Excessive pulling – by two stops or more – yields a flat, poorly defined negative and creates colour casts.

97
Don't up- or downrate a film if one with a more suitable speed rating is available – unless, that is, you specifically want to alter grain and colour rendition.

98
Don't push or pull colour negative film by more than one stop. The colour casts and distortions that may result could be impossible to correct at printing.

99
Be sure, if you're using a processing firm, to tell them if you have up- or downrated the film. Developing time can be altered to compensate, and most firms make no extra charge for this.

HOLDING CAMERAS STEADY

100
Don't make exposures when you're out of breath, on tiptoe or in any uncomfortable position. Blur caused by camera shake is probably the most common cause of disappointing pictures: it makes them fuzzy.

101
Don't stoop to take a low-angle shot. If you kneel down you will be able to hold the camera steadier.

102
Don't lean backwards when taking a photo. Kneel down, and if necessary support the lens on your forearm, as in 119.

103
Don't hold a camera gingerly by the fingertips. Use the palm of your hand as a cradle, particularly when supporting the camera from beneath if framing a picture vertically.

104
Avoid elbow-to-knee contact when supporting a camera for a low-angle shot. Your thighs make a more secure base.

105 Remember
Always relax when squeezing the trigger. Try holding your breath, or exhaling slowly.

106
Squeeze the shutter release gently. Use a soft-release button if the camera accepts one.

107
Press the camera firmly against your cheek.

108
Brace yourself against a wall or any available solid object.

109 Lightweights
Be especially careful to hold lightweight pocket cameras steady. Because using them usually needs so little concentration, camera shake is all the more likely.

110 Cradling SLRs
Hold an SLR properly by cradling the lens in the palm of the left hand, using its thumb and second finger to operate the focus and aperture rings. Grip the camera body with the right hand, using its thumb to work the wind-on lever and to act as a brace on the back of the camera while the index finger presses the trigger.

111 Disc and 110
Hold a disc camera with your fingers on the front of the body and your thumbs behind. With a 110, use the thumbs to support the camera from beneath when taking horizontally framed shots. Beware your fingers don't obscure the lens, meter or flash.

112 Vertical shots
When framing vertically, have one hand underneath the camera to take its weight while the other keeps it steady from above. Adjust your grip until you find the easiest way to operate the controls.

113 Standing firm
Tuck one or both elbows in against your ribs to give extra stability to the camera. Stand in a relaxed, balanced position with the feet apart. You should be able to pivot easily from the hips.

114 Low-angle shots
Kneel rather than crouch to take a low-angle shot – or sit cross-legged with your elbows resting on your thighs.

115 Ground-level
For these shots, lie down on your stomach and use the elbows as props.

116 Camera supports
If the picture angle allows, rest the camera on a convenient solid object. Use a rolled-up sweater or bean bag (a soft cloth bag filled with beans or expanded polystyrene chips) to act as a cushion if the surface is uneven and/or hard.

117 Improvising braces
Keep your neck-strap short, so you can lead it round a forearm, take up the slack, and brace the camera.

118
A non-stretch cord loop passed through the camera neck-strap makes a useful brace for eye-level shots. Hook the other end under either foot and pull upwards.

119
Form a brace for supporting a heavy lens by gripping your right wrist with the left hand; prop your left elbow against a wall and rest the lens on the left forearm.

120 Shutter speed
If there's no means of supporting the camera, set a shutter speed of at least 1/60 when using a standard lens, 1/125 with a 100mm or 135mm lens, and 1/250 with a 200mm. See 313.

121 Using a tripod
To raise a tripod to the correct height, extend the thickest leg sections first and then the narrow sections The further apart the legs, the more stable the tripod will be. Use the centre column only for making fine adjustments: if over-extended, it may make a lightweight tripod unstable.

122 Cable release
Always use a cable release when shooting with the camera on a tripod. Finger pressure on the release button can give shake, even if the camera seems to be firm. If you've forgotten the cable release, use the camera's self-timing device to release the shutter.

123 Tripod stiffener
Increase the stability of a tripod in strong winds by lowering its centre of gravity. Hang a camera bag, or even a bag of rocks, from the tripod so that it is suspended just above the ground.

124 Table-top tripod
It's worth carrying one of these compact, light tripods at all times. Use it in the conventional manner on suitable surfaces, or press the legs against your chest.

125
Don't use the recommended minimum shutter speeds in 120 if camera shake problems persist. Switch to higher speeds until you find one at which you produce consistently sharp pictures.

126
Don't shirk taking your tripod with you unless it's totally inconvenient to carry one. You can improve almost any shot – even at faster shutter speeds – by using a tripod. If mobility is important, a monopod is a useful alternative.

127
Be careful when opening out a tripod. Don't just release the locks and let the legs drop down – it's easy to damage a tripod this way.

128
Never pull a cable release taut – you may jerk the camera.

129
Don't screw the tripod bush into the camera body if it's fitted with one of the long, heavy telephotos. This puts unnecessary strain on the lens mount. Use the mounting ring on the lens.

EXPOSURE

130
Don't accept meter readings as gospel truth. They are mostly only reliable in straightforward lighting conditions.

131
Don't take a series of photographs, even though it is of the same subject, in what seems to be the same light without checking before each shot that you have the go-ahead from the meter. Light levels can fluctuate fast, and frequent fine adjustments may be necessary to avoid spoiling the sequence with the odd incorrectly exposed shot. (This does not apply in controlled lighting.)

132
Don't let meter batteries become run down. When their power output is low, a meter, whether hand-held or built in-to a camera, is likely to give inaccurate readings.

133 Remember
You must adjust aperture and shutter speed in tandem: they work in conjunction to control exposure. The aperture, also called the diaphragm or iris, and measured in f stops, controls the intensity of the light passing through the lens, and also the depth of field – see **171–172**. The shutter speed controls how long the film will be exposed to that light. The faster the shutter speed, the wider the corresponding aperture must be to produce the correct exposure. The slower the shutter speed, the narrower the aperture. If in doubt about what combination to choose, see **139** and **140**.

134
Take note of the speed of the film you buy. Some films are more light-sensitive than others: the higher the ISO rating on the pack, the faster, or more sensitive to light, is the film. A slow-speed film needs more exposure than a faster one in identical lighting.

135
When loading a new film into the camera you must key its ISO rating into the meter system. Every picture on the roll could be spoilt if you forget to make this vital adjustment to a camera with built-in metering.

136 Simple cameras
If your camera has no exposure control – no adjustable shutter speeds or aperture – best results will generally only be got by shooting outdoors in bright light. Indoors, use flash. However, this is only a rule of thumb – see **137**.

137 Fast film option
On dull days, in heavily overcast conditions, heavy shade or weak evening light, you can get good results from a non-adjustable camera simply by using a fast film. But remember, a fast film may give 'washed-out', overexposed pictures if you expose it in bright sunshine.

138 Exposure symbols
If you have a simple camera on which exposure is controlled by 'sunny', 'hazy' and 'cloudy' symbols, choose your setting as much by the nature and position of the subject as by the actual weather. Pictures taken in sunlight will turn out well if you use the 'sunny' setting. But if, for instance, your subject then moves to the shade – perhaps of a tree or umbrella – use the 'cloudy' setting to let in more light and so prevent an underexposed final result.

139 Shutter first?
If you have an adjustable (but non-automatic or programmed) camera, you will find the decision about which combination of aperture and shutter speed to use easier to make if you first make a basic distinction: is the subject moving or static? If it is moving, your first priority is to choose a shutter speed fast enough to freeze the action (see **214–220**).

140 Aperture first?
If depth of field – see **172** – is more important than anything else, select a suitably narrow aperture followed by the shutter speed required for correct exposure. You are most likely to enjoy this freedom when the subject is static and shutter speed consequently less critical.

141 Poor light
Before accepting the unsatisfactory combination of slow shutter speed and wide aperture forced by poor light, stop and consider ways of getting more light on to the subject: move the subject; change the camera position; get rid of obstacles in the passage of light.

142 TTL systems
Most SLRs with 'through the lens' (TTL) metering are centre-weighted: the meter cells 'read' mainly from the centre of the frame with (usually) an additional bias to the bottom half of the frame. So be careful if you are taking a vertical shot – the meter will be inclined to read more light from one side of the picture than the other. Centre-weighting is designed to give accurate readings when the subject is in the centre of the frame and sky occupies the top half.

143
If using an SLR with a centre-weighted system to take a horizontal shot in which the upper half is much darker than the lower half, either hold the camera upside down or compensate for the underexposure that would result.

144
If your SLR has an overall averaging system you may still have to compensate when a scene has emphatic light or dark areas.

145
Some SLRs have spot meters, which read just a small area in the centre of the viewfinder. So if taking a wide view, beware of any central area which is exceptionally light or dark.

146 Hand-held meters
When taking reflected light readings with a hand-held meter (i.e. meter is pointed at subject), watch out for the same sort of problems that occur with TTL systems – see **152–5**. Be especially careful not to accidentally point the meter at the sky, so getting a reading that will underexpose the rest of the scene: almost certainly the most common pitfall of this type of meter.

147
Obtain an accurate exposure for unusually contrasty, dark or light subjects by using a hand-held meter for an incident light reading. Go up to the subject; attach the diffusing dome; point the meter at the principal light source for the subject; take the reading.

149
Don't forget that if you're using a filter you'll probably have to increase the exposure. This means opening up the aperture manually or reducing the shutter speed, unless the camera has TTL metering or a meter sensor which is covered by the filter when in place.

150
Don't despair if all your pictures are over- or under-exposed. The meter calibration may be faulty. If you cannot have the camera repaired straightaway, try to estimate the extent of the error and reset the film speed dial accordingly.

151 Generally
Base your exposure reading on the main subject of the picture if the lighting is coming from roughly behind you – in other words, if the subject enjoys straightforward, frontal illumination.

152
If the subject is back-lit, or if exceptionally dark or light areas appear in the scene, it is best to go right up to the subject to take the reading. Set the camera (with some automatic models you can 'lock in' the reading) and then return to the position from which you want to take the picture. Don't worry if the meter now indicates incorrect exposure – it is being misled by the unimportant lighting elements.

153 Skies
Pictures often turn out underexposed if a large expanse of sky is included. If a camera has TTL metering, avoid this simply by tilting the camera downwards so that the meter reads more of the foreground. Then recompose and shoot.

154 Light subjects
Because meters can be misled by exceptionally light, reflective subjects filling the frame – for example a girl in a pure white dress frontally lit by direct sunlight – give about one stop more exposure than the meter indicates. You can do this either by keeping the same shutter speed and opening up to the next stop (a lower f number) or by keeping the aperture the same and changing to the next slowest shutter speed.

155 Dark subjects
For extra-dark, non-reflective subjects, follow the same procedure as in **154** but this time give one stop less exposure.

156 Compensation
Exposure adjustments as in **154** and **155** are easy to make on instant picture cameras having a lighten/darken control, and on simple cameras with weather symbol settings. Changing to 'darken' or from 'cloudy' to 'sunny' is roughly the same as giving one stop less exposure.

157
If you have a semi-automatic camera (either aperture or shutter priority), make adjustments as in **154** and **155** with the camera set on manual. But if the camera has a separate exposure compensation control, you may prefer to use this instead, with the camera set on automatic, and thus retain the camera's ability to respond instantly to changes in light.

158
Even if your camera is fully automatic, with no manual override, you can still make exposure compensations. To give one stop more exposure, turn the film speed dial to half the ISO rating of the film in the camera. To give one stop less, double the ISO rating. But remember to reset the dial to normal before the next shot.

159 Contrasty subjects
If your subject is unevenly lit, and contains significantly dark and bright areas, the meter reading may be inaccurate. If

the dark areas dominate, the exposure will probably be correct for those parts of the picture but with the highlights overexposed. And if you expose for the highlights, the darker areas will be underexposed. And if the main subject is in either the highlight or shadow areas, and it would be acceptable to lose some detail in other areas, an exposure taken directly from the subject will probably work. But if the whole scene has to be recorded in detail, measure the correct apertures for highlights and shadows, then use an f stop half-way between.

160 Grey card reading

If a subject's range of bright and dark areas is so wide that it confuses you, the meter or both, take your reading from a more evenly lit object nearby. The palm of your hand or the dull side of brown wrapping paper are fine; or you could use a special photographic grey card with an 18% tint. All represent an average subject tone. Remember that light you measure on an improvised surface like this must come from the same direction as, and be of similar intensity to, what falls on the subject.

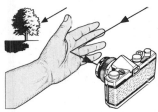

161 Bracketing

The simplest way of ensuring a perfectly exposed shot is to take a series of the same subject at slightly different exposures – bracketing. First adjust the camera to the exposure indicated by the meter, and shoot. Then make additional exposures at one and two stops over and under the meter's indicated exposure. If you feel the picture requires truly critical accuracy, use steps of half a stop. Automatic cameras should be set to manual for this procedure.

162 'Fooling' autos

To bracket with an automatic camera, use the manual override or the exposure compensation control. With fully automated cameras, adjust the film speed dial to give the equivalent of one or two stops' worth of over- or underexposure: to bracket with 200 ISO film, for example, shoot in turn with the dial at 50, 100, 200, 400 and 800 ISO.

163 Meter failure

If your meter fails to respond but the camera controls are still functioning – you can improvise exposure settings. Set the aperture to f16 and the shutter to the nearest approximation of the ISO rating of the film in use: for example, 1/60 with 64 ISO film, 1/500 with 400 ISO, and so on. This will give reasonably accurate exposure in bright sun. In hazy sun, open up to f11 (or change to the next slowest shutter speed); if it's cloudy, open up to f8; if it's heavily overcast, open up to f5.6. Add an extra stop to each increase if you're shooting in weak early morning or evening light. You may well be pleasantly surprised at results with this method.

164
Don't dismiss bracketing – see 160 – because you think it's a waste of film. Shot for shot, film is the cheapest photographic item, and a few wasted frames are better than a wasted opportunity.

165
Don't use shutter speeds longer than 1 sec when bracketing: instead, adjust the aperture. Exposures longer than 1 sec upset the normal behaviour of film and cause poor colour rendition. Special exposure calculations and filters are needed to counter these.

166
Don't forget, if you're using a shutter-priority automatic camera, that while you can easily programme a wide aperture by simply setting a fast shutter speed, you may need to set a much slower speed to gain a small aperture. And that speed could be so slow that camera shake is a problem.

167
Don't ignore the shutter speed selected by the meter when you're using an aperture-priority camera on automatic. If it's a slow shutter speed, you may have to take extra precautions to hold the camera steady.

168 Remember
The aperture (the opening made by the iris or diaphragm, and measured as an f stop) regulates the intensity of light reaching the film. You must balance it with a shutter speed that's long (or brief) enough for that light to record as a correctly exposed image on the film.

Aperture control ring
22 16 11 8 5.6 4 2.8 2

169
If you set too slow a shutter speed, and/or too wide an aperture, the picture will receive too much exposure to light. It will look pale and washed-out, with detail lost in the highlight (lightest) areas. With too fast a shutter speed, and/or too small an aperture, the picture will receive insufficient exposure. It will look dark, and the shadow areas will lose detail. However, overexposure can suggest a delicate, ethereal quality that enhances some subjects.

170
To double the intensity of light passing through the lens, move the aperture ring on the lens barrel to the next lowest f number – for example from f11 to f8. To reduce the light intensity by half, move to the next highest f stop – in this case f16. These operations are known as 'opening up' and 'stopping down' respectively.

f2.8   4   5.6   8   11   16

171 Exposure symbols
On simpler cameras – including many cartridge-loading models – aperture settings are simplified into weather symbols. 'Cloudy' is the wider aperture setting and 'sunny' the smaller.

172 Depth of field
Always be aware that the different apertures have distinct effects on depth of field – how much of the scene in front of, and behind, the point on which you have focused will come out sharp in the final result. The rule is, the smaller the aperture, the more will be sharply focused at the same distance setting. And at the same aperture, depth of field is always greater with distant subjects.

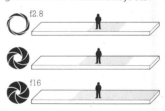
f2.8

f16

173
When exploiting depth of field, remember it extends twice as far behind the point you have focused on than it does in front of that point.

174 Simple cameras
You need not worry about depth of field on a basic camera: their optics are ranged so that everything from about 6 ft (2m) to infinity will be in focus. Depth of field extends through the whole picture, except for close-up objects, for which a supplementary lens should be used.

175 Depth of field scale

If you are good at estimating distances, and your camera has no depth of field preview (see **176**), use the scale printed on the lens barrel to discover what depth of field you have at a given aperture. Two scales of f numbers (corresponding to the aperture settings available on that lens) extend either side of the central mark which aligns against the numbers denoting distance on the focusing ring. To see how far depth of field extends in front of and behind the point of focus, read off the distance numbers against your chosen f stop for the picture.

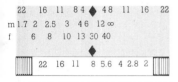

176 Preview button

Many SLRs have this useful device. Make good use of it – it's the most convenient way of judging the effect of depth of field at different apertures. Press the button (sited close to, or actually on the lens barrel) and the diaphragm will stop down to the chosen aperture (see **194**) showing you, on the reflex viewing system's screen, exactly how much of the picture will be in focus. If you don't like the effect, change to another aperture and have another look with the preview button depressed.

A slicker way of using the preview button is to focus the lens and then, with the preview button depressed, rotate the aperture ring back and forth. You will see the depth of field increasing and decreasing;

choose the right balance of sharpness and unsharpness for the creative needs of the picture. (Some readjustment to focus may be necessary so that depth of field extends over the area you want.) Now look to see what aperture is indicated by the aperture ring on the lens barrel; set the appropriate shutter speed for correct exposure, and shoot.

177 Preview button snag

At small apertures, the SLR viewfinder image may be so dark when you press the preview button that you can't see the focusing effect clearly. The only way round this is to focus the lens at full aperture on the nearest point you want sharply focused. Note the distance setting, then refocus on the furthest point you want to show up as sharp. Note this distance too, and then refer to the depth of field scale on the lens barrel (see **175**) to work out which aperture encompasses this range.

Aperture ring   Preview button

178 Selective focusing

By selecting a wide aperture you can restrict depth of field so that it extends only through a limited, but nonetheless important, part of the scene. This way you can reduce unsightly, distracting background objects to a blur if need be, at the same time concentrating the eye on the sharply focused part of the picture. This effect is most pronounced with a telephoto lens.

179

Avoid using a budget-priced lens at its widest or narrowest aperture settings. Picture sharpness with such lenses improves noticeably when they are used two or three stops down from maximum aperture.

180

Don't try to shoot a scene in which you want both close and distant objects to be sharp without carefully calculating the aperture you will need to give enough depth of field to bring both into focus.

181
Don't shoot closer
than 6ft (2m) from
your subject if you
have a simple
camera with no
focusing control
There are variations
from model to
model, but mostly
everything closer
than this will be out
of focus, even if it
looks sharp in the
viewfinder. Equally,
don't regard the
focusing symbols on
some simple
cameras as a luxury
you can ignore. You
may occasionally
get a sharp result
with the control set
wrongly, because
sometimes focusing
is not critical – see
172–178. But you
equally may not.

182 Remember
It pays to make accurate focusing a habit. If you're always
confident focusing is taken
care of – or can be easily taken
care of – it will leave you freer
to concentrate on the other
controls, as well as on creative
problems. On cameras with an
adjustable aperture, depth of
field (see **172**) may give a wide
zone of sharpness, but you
must still focus the camera accurately because then you can
easily calculate how far that
zone extends in front of and
behind your subject (see **175**).

183
Try to have the camera
roughly focused at all times. If
you have fully adjustable
focusing, as on SLRs and advanced compacts, set the
focusing ring on one of three
broad zones according to
where your next shot(s) is/are
most likely to fall: close-up,
middle distance or long distance. This leaves the smallest
possible last-minute adjustment to make for total sharpness while composing through
the viewfinder, which might
mean the difference between
achieving or missing a fleeting
picture opportunity. Lengthy
last-minute fiddling with the
focusing ring can lose you the
patience of portrait-sitters, too.

184 Symbols
Be aware of what focusing symbols actually mean. They're
generally supplied as focusing
aids on the more advanced
pocket cameras, and though
there's some variation between makes (see your instruction manual) you should generally use the landscape or view
symbol for subjects 15ft (5m) or

more from the camera. For
subjects 9–15ft (3–5m) away
use the group symbol. Anything 6–9ft (2–3m) away, use the
head and body setting. The
portrait symbol is for subjects
at 3–6ft (1–2m). If in doubt about
what symbol covers a subject,
use these distances.

185 Rangefinders
When using a rangefinder
focusing system, generally a
feature of the more sophisticated 35mm compact cameras,
make sure the rangefinder spot
is targeted on the subject, or
whatever part of it needs to be
the point of focus. This is particularly true if a foreground
subject is off-centre, so that the
spot falls on a background
area.

Focus on subject   Recompose

186 Difficulty focusing?
If you find focusing with a
rangefinder or reflex camera
difficult, try rotating the focusing ring back and forth each
side of the approximate point
of focus in ever-decreasing
arcs until the image is sharp.

187 Practice
If you've just acquired an SLR,
keep practising with the focusing system. It is one of the
camera's prime features. Appreciate the fact that it allows
you to watch the whole image
move in and out of focus, and,
by depressing the preview
button (if there is one – see **176**)
to examine which areas of the
picture will be sharp, or not.

188 Composition

Whenever you focus, consider which parts of the scene need to be sharply focused and which don't. The eye is automatically drawn to the part of the scene which appears sharpest; it's easy to achieve impact by deliberately rendering some parts of the scene – typically backgrounds – in soft focus. See **178**.

189 SLR focusing aids

Get the best results from an SLR's central focusing area, with its various facilities, by using them on the subjects for which they work best. The split image arrangement comes into its own if a subject has well-defined 'lines'. For textured surfaces, without prominent straight lines, use the cluster of microprisms; if the surface is out of focus, they make it look scrambled; in focus, it looks normal.

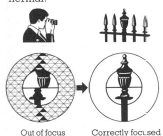

Out of focus   Correctly focused

190 Changing screens

Some find split image and/or microprism focusing aids at the centre of SLR viewfinders distracting. Check whether your camera accepts interchangeable focusing screens and, if so, try using a plain one. See **193**. Other types of focusing screen may solve further viewing problems – see **191, 192**.

191 Grid pattern screen

If your camera accepts interchangeable screens, and you do plenty of work requiring perfectly squared-up angles, such as document copying, or photographing buildings, it is probably worth buying a screen marked with a grid pattern – extremely helpful for the purpose

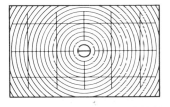

192 Extra microprisms

Special screens with a larger than standard area of microprisms may be available for your camera if it accepts interchangeable screens. They make focusing easier in low light levels, but make sure such a screen is matched to the focal length of the lens.

193 Plain screen

If your camera takes interchangeable screens, and you often do critical close-up work, or shoot with long lenses, a plain screen could be useful. The absence of split-image or microprism focusing aids leaves you free to concentrate on composition. And microprism screens designed for use with standard lenses tend to be rendered useless by telephotos: the relatively narrow maximum apertures of such lenses tend to make the prisms black out – a real drawback because telephotos usually need critical focusing (**309**).

194
Don't forget that with an SLR you normally compose and focus pictures with the lens at full aperture. Unless you've adjusted the aperture to its widest possible setting, it will automatically stop down after you press the shutter release. This makes depth of field (see **172-178**) increase. Parts of the picture which you saw as out of focus on the viewing screen could well come out sharp in the final result. Use the preview button (see **176** and **177**) to check what will be in and out of focus.

FOCUSING PROBLEMS

195
Beware when taking a picture of a reflection with a non-reflex camera. You must focus on the image being reflected – not cn the reflective surface. Create extra depth of field by stopping down if you want zones in front of and behind the main reflected subject to be sharp too.

196 Remember
Autofocus cameras have limitations (see **43**), and while they leave you free to concentrate on other things, if a subject is out of the ordinary, it may be better to focus manually, or use the memory lock.

197 In the air
If you find it difficult to focus continuously on a subject moving through the air, or on water, where there are no obvious reference points, try this procedure. First, pick up the subject in the viewfinder while it is still some distance off, and focus sharply. Then, as the subject moves on, pull the focus *past* it. As the subject passes through this new point, it will become sharp again. Now pull the focus further on again, and continue doing so, keeping slightly ahead of the subject. When the subject looks just about right in the viewfinder, pull the focus past the subject once more, and when the two converge, shoot.

198 Ground level
For ground-level shots where you have reference points – a fence or a tree perhaps – before you shoot a moving subject select a reference point it will pass close by and focus on that. Track the subject in the viewfinder and, when it reaches the point, shoot.

199 Angled views
When photographing a subject from an angle (and especially if shooting at a wide aperture) you may find that while the front of the subject is in focus, the rear is increasingly un-sharp. To avoid this effect, focus not on the obvious nearest point but instead about a third of the way back along its length. Depth of field extends about twice as far behind a subject as in front, so your depth of field will range correctly over as much of the subject as your aperture allows.

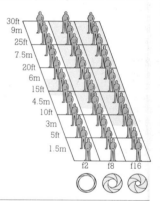

200 In the dark
If there are no bright points to focus on in a dimly lit or night-time shot, get someone to hold a match or candle close to the subject and focus on this instead.

201 Zooms
If you own a 'one touch' zoom – with the controls for focusing and zooming (changing the focal length) on the same ring – double check focus when you finish zooming and before you shoot. It's easy to slightly alter the focus while zooming.

202 Always

Cut out the clutter before you press the shutter. Too many pictures are filled with pointless detail and too few people notice it because they're concentrating exclusively on the main image in the viewfinder. A camera records everything it's pointed at, not just what you think interesting.

203

Systematically inspect all four sides of the viewfinder while composing shots. Regard the viewfinder as a frame – not only for getting things in but leaving them out.

204

Look through the viewfinder square-on; make sure you can see all four sides. If you peer through at an angle, you may cut out part of the scene.

205 Eyesight correction

If you wear glasses, buy an appropriate eyesight correction lens to fit over the eyepiece – then you can remove your glasses and get your eye right up against the viewfinder.

206 Coming in close

As a rule of thumb, it's usually better to come in to where you feel uncomfortably close to the subject than to move back until it fits neatly inside the frame. The first sort of shot will probably have punch; the second won't.

207

It's doubly important to come in close if your subject's small and the background fussy.

208 'Magic' frame

Framing pictures well is so basic to good photography that it's worth practising with a dummy. Just cut a frame from a piece of card to the proportions of your viewfinder

209 Cropping

Remember the image recorded on the film is slightly larger in area than that seen through many viewfinders. Make allowances for this if framing is critical; and remember machine-made prints are cropped slightly.

210 Parallax

If you have a non-reflex camera – which includes most simple pocket and compact cameras – beware of parallax. This is the error due to the different viewpoints of the lens and the viewfinder. In the final picture, subjects can in theory be off-centre and cut away at the top. Parallax is usually no problem, however, because either the viewfinder is corrected for the error (except at extreme close range), or guidelines appear inside the viewfinder. But see **211**.

211 Close-up parallax

Parallax (**210**) can be a problem with close-ups in the 4–6ft (1–2m) range. If a camera lacks correction marks, or you need to make doubly certain a subject is all in the frame, make your own correction simply by noting the position of the viewfinder in relation to the lens. Ensure that the subject is well clear of the viewfinder edge where the error could occur; for example, keep heads well clear of the top.

212

Never just photograph a subject from where you happen to be standing – without first moving around looking at the effects of different viewpoints. You'd be surprised how some subjects gain stature when simply seen from another viewpoint. And this can affect the way you frame a picture.

213
Don't expect good results of all moving subjects if your camera has just one shutter speed or a limited range of speeds – say 1/30 to 1/250. A disc camera's shutter fires at 1/100 or 1/200 sec only; other pocket cameras may work at 1/60. That may seem a very short time indeed, but it is long enough for a walking figure 10ft (3m) away from the camera to record as a blur on film. With these cameras, try to restrict yourself to static or slow-moving subjects; or try panning – see **219**.

214 Remember
Shutter speed controls the length of time light from the subject is projected on to the film. Which shutter speed you choose matters most when photographing moving subjects. All the time the shutter is open, the image moves across the film. The faster the shutter speed, the less the image moves while the shutter is open. Blurred pictures result if the shutter is open too long: motion is recorded on the film.

1/60

1/30

215 Rule of thumb
Assuming a subject is in the middle distance, moves not straight across but diagonally through your field of view, and you're using a standard lens, you can quite simply estimate the shutter speed needed to freeze its motion. First estimate the subject's speed, for example 20mph (32km/h) for a man running, 50 mph (80km/h) for a car, 100mph (160km/h) for a racing car. Multiply this figure by ten: then select the shutter speed that corresponds to

the result. The running man would require 1/250; the car 1/500 and the racing car 1/1000. If there is no exact equivalent, use the next highest speed.

216 Direction of motion
If the subject is approaching the camera head-on, halve the speed calculated by the method explained in **215**.

217
If the subject is moving directly from one side of the frame to the other, quadruple the shutter speed calculated by the method in **215** – i.e. select two speed settings faster.

218 Full frame action
You must use much faster shutter speeds than given in **215** if a subject occupies most of the frame, either because you're close to it or because you are using a telephoto lens. Generally, shoot at two speed settings higher than described in **215**. The walking man, for example, shot from 6ft (2m) should record sharp at 1/1000.

219 Panning
If you've got a simple camera with a fixed shutter speed, or are forced to use a slow shutter speed because the light is poor, try panning. Stand firmly, so you can pivot smoothly from the hips; tuck your elbows well into your sides; line up the subject in the viewfinder, pre-focus, and follow it in a steady, smooth movement. When you think it's well framed, shoot, and don't stop following through. The background will be blurred, the subject sharp.

220 Peak of action

Capitalize on the fact that many types of action have a 'dead' point which can be frozen by a relatively slow shutter speed. A pole vaulter, for instance, hangs almost motionless in the air for an instant as he clears the bar, as does a footballer having risen to head the ball or a diver after leaving the springboard. You may well freeze these climactic moments with shutter speeds of 1/125, 1/60 or even 1/30. And a sense of motion could be conveyed far better than by perfectly freezing the action, which can look boringly static.

221 Deliberate blur

Blur caused by camera shake will ruin a picture. Blur caused by subject movement may, if used the right way, suggest an impression of speed and motion. So try using deliberately slow speeds: they can give life to action pictures. Choose a background to offset the blur.

222 Streaking highlights

Blurring caused by subject movement records as streaks of light on film. The length of each streak doubles with each progressively slower speed used. Experiment with various shutter speeds to see what kind of 'speed lines' you can create with different subjects.

223 Slow speeds

If you are deliberately using a slow speed for effect, remember not to go slower than the minimum safe speeds if hand-holding the camera. If you mount the camera on a tripod or firmly support it in some other way and use a cable release, you can use the camera's whole range of shutter speeds, regardless of what lens is in place.

224 ND filters

If you want to use a slow shutter speed but the light is too bright or your film is too fast – even with the lens fully stopped down – use neutral density (ND) filters. Without affecting colour or contrast, they reduce the intensity of light passing through the lens, acting like smaller apertures (higher f numbers).

225
Don't give up on an action shot in seemingly impossible conditions without first considering the alternatives: switching to a faster film or uprating; moving away from the subject; changing the viewpoint; switching to a shorter focal length lens with a wider maximum aperture and later enlarging a portion of the image. In facing light you can prolong the time in which you can operate by shooting the subject in silhouette against the evening sky.

226
Keep an eye on the shutter speed selected by an aperture-priority automatic camera. It may not be fast enough to freeze movement, in which case you should open up the lens wider.

227
If using flash, **check** that the shutter speed selected preserves the synchronization. If in doubt, see **254**.

AVAILABLE LIGHT

228
Don't confine your picture taking to bright sunlight – even if you have the simplest type of camera with no exposure control. You can always load a fast film – see **64** and **83**. Strong sunlight creates deep, unflattering shadows.

229
Don't take portrait photographs in bright sunlight at noon. The sun directly overhead lights the top of the head and the tip of the nose, leaving the rest in shadow. To avoid an awful result, shoot in the shade, or use a reflector to put light into the face.

230
Never give up taking pictures because you think the light is too poor. See **91** and **141** for ideas on overcoming low light exposure problems; think creatively; exploit poor light to produce original images in unusual conditions.

231 Remember
Lighting is at least as important as any subject: no light, no photograph; interesting light, interesting photograph.

232 Matching light
Constantly search for light that is appropriate to your subjects. Bright sun is right for beach shots; a distant range of mountains could look its best dramatically shrouded in cloud, or against a backdrop of black storm sky.

233 Changing light
Be continually alert to the way light changes – sometimes from minute to minute. Its direction, intensity, ability to light a subject adequately, the way it brings out form, texture and colour must all be considered, all the time.

234
Make allowances when the light changes. On the most basic level, this means changing position so light falls more evenly on the subject.

235 Come back later
Be prepared to come back another time if you think the lighting will be better.

236 Time of day
Get up early to take pictures – and stay out late – particularly in the hotter latitudes. Dawn and dusk lay fair claim to providing the most interesting light of the whole 24 hours.

237 Experiment
To gain a better understanding of the changing quality of light through the day, photograph a familiar building in colour every hour from dawn to dusk. The range of colours and qualities may surprise you.

238 Dawn
Use the crisp, sharp light of dawn to photograph objects which later in the day may be obscured by shadows. Ektachrome will emphasize the prominent blue tones produced by light at this time, creating an impression of tranquillity in landscape photographs.

239 Sunrise
When you've made the effort to rise at dawn, hang around for true sunrise rather than go home for breakfast. The light of a clear sunrise is warm and romantic, low and directional, picking out objects in a dramatic way as they catch the sun, and creating interesting shadows. Shoot quickly: the light's angle changes rapidly; the sun touches the horizon for less than 90 seconds.

240 Mid-morning
By this time you should think of moving portrait subjects into shade – contrast could be too harsh, as also in the open, landscape shot. Colours record conventionally now, however.

241 Afternoon
Pick the late afternoon for informal, outdoor portraits. The increasingly golden light flatters skin tones. The sunlight is generally softer, restoring form and texture after the harsh light of midday.

242 Evening
At sunset the light level falls quicker than many people expect, so plan your shots and keep an eye on exposure. As sunsets progress, the light is increasingly reddish – not always flattering – and large areas may have uncomfortably deep shadows.

243 Light direction
If you want to record maximum detail and the most intense colour, lighting should come from the front. But remember you may achieve these at the expense of suggesting form.

244 Side-lighting
Has its drawbacks – see 251 – but the play of shadows it often creates can give useful modelling – display of shape. Other uses of side-lighting are emphasis of texture, and the 'mysterious' portrait with one half of the face in shadow.

245 Backlighting
Achieve a silhouette, or near-silhouette effect by backlighting a subject. Shape is emphasized, but colour, texture and detail are restricted. Take care with exposure – see 152.

246 Rimlighting
To achieve a halo effect, place the subject directly between a bright light source and the camera. Experiment with different positions.

247 Reflectors
Reveal detail in shadow areas of side- or backlit subjects by positioning a reflector – a sheet of white card serves well – so it reflects light into the dark areas. The further the reflector from the subject, the weaker the effect. This is a basic technique for any light source.

248 Diffuse light
To emphasize overall form and modelling use soft, diffused light, as created when the sun is filtered by clouds or rain. In this type of light, colours are muted, the transition from directly lit to shadow areas is gradual, and you can rely on automatic exposure readings.

249 Indoors
Try shooting portraits indoors by available light. There's more illumination close to windows than you might expect, and it's softer than artificial light or flash.

250
Be careful when including windows and open doorways in available light shots taken indoors. They are likely to create excessive contrast, with resulting problems in balancing exposure between highlight and shadow areas.

251
Avoid side-lighting if a subject's shape means some of it will be brilliantly lit while other parts are hidden by shadow. It is difficult balancing exposure for such shots. Portraits commonly suffer from this type of lighting defect.

252
Don't shoot full-face portraits with a flashgun mounted on the camera, pointing straight at the subject, in line with the axis of the lens. At short distances this causes the 'red eye' effect – a result of light directly illuminating the retinas, whose surfaces are covered with blood vessels. Bounce the light off a wall or ceiling instead, or take the flash off the camera, connecting it with an extension lead. If this is not possible, shine a torch into the subject's face to contract the pupils just before releasing the shutter.

253
Don't fire flash at highly reflective surfaces such as mirrors. They bounce light away so efficiently that parts of the picture can be 'whited out', and/or exposure radically altered.

254
Don't use electronic flash at shutter speeds with which it cannot synchronize. On cameras with focal plane shutters, this is normally 1/125 sec.

255 Remember
Flash is not just for indoors or where light is dim. Use it to freeze movement, fill shadows and for special effects.

256 The distance factor
Automatic flash on pocket and instant picture cameras is mostly foolproof, but be cautious if using a film that is much faster or slower than the one specified for use with the flash. To obtain correct exposure, you may need to alter your distance from the subject. This is because flash intensity falls off by a factor of four with each doubling of distance from the unit.

257
Because flash intensity falls off the further the light travels from the unit, group pictures need special care. Bunch the subjects tightly, otherwise those nearer the camera will come out brighter.

258 Simple flash
Low-power units, such as those fitted to pocket, simple compacts and many instant picture cameras, work best on subjects 3–10ft (1–3m) from the camera. Any nearer, the subject will probably be 'bleached out'; further, it will come out dark. However, you can extend the upper limit of flash by loading with faster film.

259 Ready lights
With many flashguns, the signal indicating the unit is ready to fire will come on when the unit is only 50–70% charged. If time allows, give it an extra 5–10 secs to come to full power.

260 Flash exposure
If you have a flashgun with a power output not automatically regulated, you have to vary the aperture setting depending on the distance of subject from camera. Use the chart or table usually mounted on such units; film speed has to be taken into account, too.

261 Guide numbers
For flash-to-subject distances greater or less than those marked on the chart/calculator dial of a manual (i.e. non-automatic) flashgun, estimate aperture using the units guide number (GN). You find the GN – listed for a range of film speeds – in the instructions for the flashgun. Divide this number by the distance between camera and subject; the resulting number corresponds to the correct aperture on 100 ISO film. See also **262.**

262
Be sure to use the correct guide number when calculating flash exposure. Sometimes two numbers are specified for films – one if the distance is reckoned in metres, the other for feet. Exposure will be wrong if you mix them up.

263 Manual flash at night
A useful rough formula for using non-automatic flashguns in

darkness outdoors (no help from room reflection) is to give 1½ stops extra exposure above what the chart suggests.

264 Auto flash at night
If using an automatic flash in darkness outdoors (i.e. no help from room reflection), compensate by halving the maximum flash-to-subject distance that the chart recommends If there is some general lighting, indoors or out, trust the automatic system to compute exposure accurately.

265 Film choice
If using electronic flash, flash bulbs or cubes (which are blue-tinted), load daylight film. If you want to expose tungsten film with flash, you must use an orange (85B) filter, mounted either on the lens or the flash unit.

266 Watch the angle
Fired directly at a subject, head-on, flash gives a harsh, uncompromising illumination, and can create unattractive, heavy shadows behind the subject. Avoid both problems by changing the angle between flash and subject, or by diffusing the light from the flash. See **267–270, 277** and **281**.

267 Bounced flash
The simple antidote to harsh, ugly flash (see **266**) is the bounce technique. It gives softer, more even lighting than direct flash, bringing out modelling. Angle the flash so it fires at the ceiling or a wall. Select an angle that gives even illumination See **268** and **270**. See also **272**.

268 Minimum power
With subjects about 6–10ft (2–3m) away and in rooms of average dimensions – ceilings around 9ft (3m) high – the minimum power of unit that will give adequate illumination when bounced is one with a guide number of 20–24 (ASA/100m). Bouncing consumes up to four stops of light. In large rooms much more power is required.

269 Bouncing with manuals
To calculate exposure for bounced flash with a manual (non-automatic) unit, add the distance from the flash to the reflective surface to the distance from the reflective surface to the subject. Divide this distance into the guide number (see **261**), then divide by two to find the f number.

270 Corner bounce
At close range, bouncing off the ceiling may give an unpleasing, top-lit effect. Try bouncing from a corner.

Bounced from ceiling

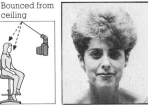

Bounced from corner

271
Don't use flash in smoky rooms – the image takes on a milky, washed-out appearance. Wait for the atmosphere to clear, or come back another time.

272
Avoid using bounced flash on dark, dirty surfaces, or when a reflective surface is remote from the flash and camera position. The bounce will not provide enough illumination.

FLASH

273
Beware of brightly coloured surfaces near your subject when using flash. Light reflected off these can produce casts of similar colours on what you are photographing.

274
Don't attempt to cover a large area when simulating sunlight (**290**) with flash. Unless you possess a powerful gun, the fall-off in light intensity as it travels will give uneven results.

275 Precautions
It's best to bracket exposure (see **161**) when using a manual unit to bounce flash. This is because the precise amount of light reflected from surfaces varies considerably. Up to two stops over- or underexposure are regularly necessary.

276
If using an automatic unit for bounced flash, make sure the flash sensor points directly at the subject. It computes exposure by measuring light reflected back to it.

277 Umbrella reflector
A purpose-made white or silver flash umbrella, or a collapsible silver reflector, or an improvised reflector – see **279** – can be used instead of a wall or ceiling as the reflective surface for bounced flash. Have a companion hold the card above the flash.

Collapsible reflector   Silver umbrella

278
To achieve softest lighting with umbrella flash, position the umbrella (or card) well away from the flash unit.

279 Makeshift reflectors
Experiment with small reflectors (white card serves well) to throw flashlight on to otherwise poorly lit parts of the subject, and pick out details.

280 Reduced output
All flash units tend to overexpose if the subject is too close. To cut light output, so lessening this effect, cover the flash with a clean white cloth. Make sure the cloth does not cover the sensor of an automatic unit, or overexposure will result.

281 Diffused flash
To soften the harsh shadows that result from direct flash, try holding a cloth two inches (5cm) or so in front of the flash. This is a useful alternative to bouncing, but note the precaution in **280**.

282 With wide-angles
If using a wide-angle lens, the wide field of view may not be covered and/or evenly illuminated by flash. To counter this, put a diffusing cloth over the flash unit as in **281**. A purpose-made wide-angle diffuser is, however, more reliable.

283 Exposure adjustment
If diffusing flash from a manual unit with a piece of cloth, it is best to bracket exposure (see **161**), especially if using the technique for the first time. Exact compensation depends on the density of the cloth being used – so experiment.

284 Off-camera flash

If you can fit a synchronization cord between flash unit and the camera's flash socket or flash shoe, experiment with off-camera flash. Mount the unit on a tripod, or hold it at arm's length. You can vary the direction of the flash light, and the way shadows fall. Bouncing and diffusing off-camera flash (**268** and **281**) further extends possibilities.

285 Predicting results

You'll want to gauge what kind of effects are produced by positioning flash off-camera, so mount an ordinary household bulb in a holder, fit a long flex and experiment before shooting the picture.

286 Fill-in flash

Use flash outdoors to supplement existing light, lighten shadows and reduce contrast. Match the effect to the existing lighting, otherwise the result will look artificial To calculate exposure, see **287**.

287 Fill-in exposure

To calculate exposure for fill-in flash outdoors, use the following procedure. In bright sunlight, set the film speed on the flashgun to double the true speed of the film in the camera. Then use the most powerful flash output option available – in other words, when the unit offers a choice of apertures, pick the smallest and set this on the camera Now use the camera's meter, or a hand-held one, to determine the shutter speed which will match this aperture – taking care to preserve camera-flash synchronization – see **254**.

288

A simple way of computing exposure when using basic flash units for outdoor fill-in is to work out the aperture using the guide number (**261**) in the normal way. Set this on the camera and then work out the shutter speed required to give correct exposure in daylight. Set this. Point the flash at the shadow area and take the picture with a cloth over the flash as in **281**.

289 Foreground subjects

With a manual gun, you can make fill-in flash stronger on a foreground subject by moving in closer. To let existing light dominate the scene, reduce the flash power, or diffuse it. To be safe, bracket (**161**) by varying the flash power.

290 Simulated sun

Fill-in flash is useful even in the soft lighting given by overcast weather. In these conditions, pictures lack sparkle, but a flash puts brilliant highlights on the eyes and other reflective surfaces. Choose the lighting angle carefully (flash must be off-camera – **284**) and remember that flash intensity falls off sharply with distance – **256**. To calculate exposure, measure the existing light, and work out the correct exposure for flash. Make bracketed exposures (**161**) around the midway point between both readings.

291

Don't overdo fill-in flash effects unless you want unusual lighting. Bracketing in steps of half a stop is the best way to achieve a natural result, similar to the effect of daylight itself. See **290**.

292
Beware of too much detail intruding in fish-eye or ultra wide-angle shots: it makes them look cluttered. Unless the subject is close to the lens and the background simple, the eye can be overpowered by the mass of visual information packed in by these lenses.

293
Don't automatically change from a wide-angle to a longer focus lens if you need to bring a subject closer – and especially if this means missing a shot. If you take the picture with the wide-angle, it can if necessary be enlarged and/or cropped at the processing stage to bring out the most interesting parts.

294 Fish-eye
Unless you want a 180° angle of view for some specific technical application, you will find the creative potential of these extreme wide-angle lenses limited. An add-on fish-eye attachment gives the circular image effect more cheaply, though with some loss of image quality. Stop down to get better results.

Add-on fish-eye

295
A full-frame fish-eye lens gives a rectangular rather than a circular image, and you can reduce its distorting effects by keeping straight lines well clear of the frame's edges.

296 Ultra wide-angle
Use these lenses (their focal lengths range from 15 to 20mm in the 35mm format) when you have an extremely confined space in which to work, or need to create the impression of space.

297
Get the most out of ultra wide-angle lenses' great creative potential by exploiting their huge depth of field and dramatic effect on perspective. Use the distortion at the edge of the frame to create interesting shapes – circles will turn into ovals, for instance, and straight lines will bend. Experiment with viewpoints until you find the most exciting effect.

298 Reducing distortion
Provided a wide-angle is sound in itself – free of aberrations – you can keep edge distortion to a minimum by holding the camera level, so that the lens and subject planes are parallel. Avoid having straight lines close to the edge of the frame. This will help preserve the square lines of, for example, an interior, without perspective 'flying away' at the edges.

299 Wide-angle – 24mm
For wide coverage of crowded, confined spaces, use a 24mm wide-angle on a 35mm camera. This lens offers an extra 10° angle of view over a 28mm (generally the step up) and significantly more depth of field. It has distortion, but most regard this as manageable. Emphasize distortion by shooting from a low or high viewpoint, minimize it by keeping everything square. With the 24mm, strong foregrounds are emphasized, distracting ones 'pushed' towards the horizon.

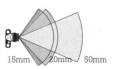

15mm   20mm   50mm

300 Wide-angle – 28mm

A 28mm gives noticeably less distortion than a 24mm, but even so, try to keep faces and other circular shapes away from the edge of the frame, otherwise they will be un-naturally elongated. Be wary, too, of the lens's ability to make verticals converge: the top of a skyscraper, for instance, will seem to recede almost to a point if the camera is tilted up at it. Equally, remember this distorting effect can be used to create dramatic compositions. The simple remedies for un-wanted distortion are moving away from the subject and changing to a longer focal length.

301 Perspective control

If you do plenty of architectural work on a 35mm camera, or frequently find situations where it is vital for all angles to be square (this includes much close-up work), consider a perspective control (PC) or shift lens. The front element can be shifted upwards or down-wards to correct or alter ver-tical or horizontal perspective – that is, perspective in a similar plane to the film.

302 Wide-angles – 35mm

Use this lens to 'pull' a subject away from its background while still keeping a visual con-nection between the two. No need to worry about edge distortion with a 35mm lens.

303 Standard lens

To record perspective in much the same way as the human eye sees it, use a standard lens. Perspective is exagger-ated with a wide-angle, com-pressed with a telephoto. See also 311.

304

If you have to shoot in really poor light, your first choice of lens is likely to be a standard lens: they're usually made with a wider maximum aperture than any other focal length in the range. On moderately priced camera systems, the standard lens will probably give better definition than other focal lengths.

305 Macro

When sharp close-ups are the main aim, a macro lens comes into its own: it is designed to operate at close range, and you can achieve life-size or larger magnifications of small objects. If a standard lens is us-ed at or near its closest focus-ing range, definition may not be up to usual standard.

Macros usually have slower maximum apertures than or-dinary standard lenses, which may limit their use in poor light; however, using macros at full aperture is unlikely because depth of field is wafer-thin in the macro range. Otherwise, use a macro just as a standard.

With standard lens   With macro lens

306

Don't rule out wide-angles for certain types of portraiture and general shots of people. A short telephoto is the ideal conventional choice (see 311), but for informal studies, or when you want to relate subject to background, the sense of immediacy and involvement created by a wide-angle is unique.

307

Don't use the lens hood belonging to your standard lens on a wide-angle – it may well cut into the image area, darkening the corners. Buy one specifically designed for the lens in use.

308
Don't expect a short telephoto lens to give the same dramatic compression of perspective you often see in telephoto shots – that is unless the picture elements are very close to each other, and to the camera. You need at least a 200mm to produce the classically powerful telephoto lens shot.

309
Never ignore depth of field when working with telephoto lenses. The longer the lens, the less depth of field (see **172**) is available at any given aperture and distance setting. Lack of depth of field is particularly acute at close range.

310
Be careful not to use the wrong size of lens hood with a telephoto. If it's too small in diameter, it will intrude in the picture: if it's too shallow, it won't do its job of shading the lens from the stray rays of light that cause flare.

311 Short telephotos
Use them first and foremost for portraits: most human faces look best in pictures where the perspective is slightly flattened. Standing say 3ft (1m) from the subject shooting with a standard lens it is possible to fill the frame, but a prominent nose or other jutting features come out unnaturally large. A longer lens enables you to stand back, achieve flatter perspective, but still fill the frame. The short telephotos, ranging from 85mm to 135mm for 35mm cameras, have shallower depth of field than standard lenses, which is another portraiture bonus. Fussy backgrounds are easier to subdue, too; see **178**.

312
Though short telephotos are often called portrait lenses – see **311** – remember they have other uses. Their gentle compression of perspective interestingly 'tightens' many a landscape shot. Equally, they come into their own when photographing details or small objects in which all the angles need to be square, and shapes distortion free.

313 Camera shake
With all telephotos, and especially the medium and longer ones, there is a minimum shutter speed to prevent blurred results through camera shake when hand holding. It corresponds roughly to the focal length, i.e. for a 105mm, 1/125; for a 200 mm, 1/250, for a 400mm, 1/500 second.

314 Medium telephoto
At 200mm, you'll begin to feel you're using a lens with 'power'; unapproachable subjects like football players will start having impact on the focusing screen. Many wildlife professionals say only with a 300mm can you properly 'approach' shyer species; but a 200mm will certainly serve you well in safari or similar situations, where closer views are possible.

315 Moving subjects
It's easy to lose moving subjects when tracking them with a long lens, so use both eyes – one peering through the viewfinder, the other observing where the subject is likely to go next.

316 Remember
A telephoto may make the focusing aids in an SLR viewfinder black out. See 193.

317 Poor light
Try to anticipate poor lighting conditions when going out with a 200mm or longer telephoto. The minimum speeds at which you can hand hold – see 313 – are rather fast. If the light is poor, you could be forced to use an uncomfortably wide aperture, perhaps with loss of definition if the lens is cheap, and certainly great restriction on depth of field. The simple answer, realized often too late, is a fast film. Pack a spare one.

318 Tripod
It is practically always worth taking a tripod for use with a long telephoto. The 300mm and 400mm lenses are surprisingly bulky – not only difficult to hand hold without shake, but inconvenient and tiring because of the weight of glass in their construction. If without a tripod, make full use of improvised supports as in 108, 115, 116, 117–119 and 124.

319 Super telephoto
There is usually no alternative to mounting a lens longer than 500mm on a tripod – unless it's a catadioptric or 'mirror' lens – see 320. If you have to be mobile, improvise with a monopod, but try to use as fast a shutter speed as possible. If possible, use two tripods – one attached to the mounting socket fitted as standard to such long lenses, the other screwed into the camera body. This is particularly worthwhile if the weather is windy. Super telephotos are widely used by professionals in sport and wildlife work, and to create dramatic bunching-up of perspective in landscapes, but generally their use is restricted by bulk.

320
If you want a super telephoto, but it has to be compact, the answer is a catadioptric or mirror lens. Bulk and length is drastically reduced by a system of internal mirrors. A 'cat' of 500mm is readily portable – but see 882, 883 and 884. The drawback is the fixed aperture, restricting depth of field and making it impossible to use the lens with shutter-priority auto exposure cameras.

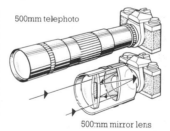

500mm telephoto

500mm mirror lens

321
Catadioptrics give characteristic doughnut-shaped highlights; if you want to imitate the effect with any conventional telephoto, just stick a coin-sized disc of black card on to a clear filter and shoot with this in place.

322 Contrast
To combat the fall-off in light at the edge of the frame when using a catadioptric, and also the reduced contrast, try pushing the film – see 92–93 and 96.

323
Take great care handling catadioptric lenses – their complex internal construction, using mirrors to shorten the length of the lens, means they are easy to damage.

324
Be on guard against atmospheric haze when using a long lens. The magnification exaggerates haze effects, so keep a skylight filter in place at all times if the camera's loaded with colour film, or an orange or red filter with b/w.

325
Don't use a zoom lens for critical work in preference to a prime lens of equivalent focal length – it will not give such a well-defined image.

326
Beware of losing focus when shooting with a 'one touch' zoom. See **201**.

327
Make sure that an add-on lens hood will shield a zoom effectively at all focal lengths before you buy it.

328 Remember
Zoom lenses have an adjustable range of focal lengths. They are most useful when you need to photograph a moving subject from a fixed position – such as at a football match, or when trying to get pictures of wild animals from a hide.

329
Although a zoom can do the work of two or more lenses of fixed focal length, even the best-quality zooms never give the same degree of resolution as equivalent prime lenses.

330 Which zoom?
Use an 80–210 zoom, or one in this range, for all kinds of action photography.

331
A zoom lens in the 28–50mm range is more useful than an 80–200mm lens if you take plenty of close-in shots (e.g. in photojournalism and travel).

80–200mm

28–50mm

332
Portrait photographers will usually find a 70–150mm the best zoom lens for their work.

333 Metering
Use the zoom lens at its maximum focal length to take exposure readings on small areas of the subject before photographing them with the lens at an intermediate setting.

334
Use the zoom control to cut out large areas of sky which might mislead the meter.

335 Focusing
Focus a zoom lens at its maximum focal length (where depth of field is shallowest), pinpointing the main subject. Then pull back to the focal length you want to use.

336 Special effects
Produce exciting special effects by zooming while the shutter is open, or use the zoom in conjunction with the pan and tilt movements of the tripod head. Try multiple exposures at different focal lengths. Use speeds lower than 1/60.

337 Macro zoom
A zoom lens used in macro mode will give a closer minimum focusing distance, but stop well down and, if possible, shoot from a tripod, for optical performance is never as good as with a true macro lens.

338 Shutter speed
If you zoom in from a short focal length to a longer one you may need to change to a higher shutter speed because image magnification governs the minimum shutter speed you must use to reduce the effect of camera shake. See **218**.

339 Flare
When photographing backlit subjects with a zoom, look out for unwanted flare. You may need to change the camera position slightly to avoid or reduce it.

340 Generally
Regard a teleconverter attachment as an alternative to buying a telephoto lens. It fits between the camera body and a
standard (or telephoto) lens.

341
A teleconverter will make
your prime lens much more
powerful. A ×2 converter will
double its focal length – but it
will also reduce any aperture
selected by two stops.

342 Improving quality
Disguise the poorer image
produced by a teleconverter
by using a soft-focus filter.

343
Compensate for the loss of contrast caused by a teleconn-
verter by pushing the film or
(with b/w) by suitable filters.

344 Framing
When using a teleconverter,
keep the subject to the centre
of the frame – definition tends
to fall off at the edges.

345
Make deliberate use of teleconverter image diffusion by
selective focusing (178) to introduce an out-of-focus background. The same applies to its
reduced depth of field.

346 Aperture
Since teleconverters reduce
the effective aperture width by
the same amount as their own
conversion factor (see 341),
take precautions (e.g. load a
fast film) against slow apertures and shutter speeds.

347 Advantage
Capitalize on the fact that a
teleconverter does not alter
how close you can focus a lens:
the closest focusing distance of
the prime lens is retained. As
prime lenses have longer minimum focusing distances the
longer their focal length, this
can be a distinct bonus. You
can for instance come in closer
with a 100mm lens fitted with a
teleconverter than with a
prime 200mm telephoto. And
this in turn can save the need to
make selective enlargements
of some key part of the image.

348
Resist buying or
using teleconverters
not intended for your
own make of lens. A
well-matched
teleconverter will
give less noticeable
fall-off in image
quality than a cheap
or ill-matched one.

200mm telephoto   100mm telephoto plus ×2 converter

349
Don't let filters lie loose in a pocket or camera bag – they scratch more easily than many people expect, and they get dusty – both of which impair image quality. See **919–920**.

350
Don't touch the surface of a filter: greasy smears are surprisingly hard to remove. Follow the maker's instructions on cleaning if you do accidentally mark a filter in this way.

351 Remember
Filters are easiest to use with an SLR camera because you can judge their effect through the viewfinder. And a built-in TTL meter automatically makes any adjustment to exposure needed as a result of a filter reducing the amount of light reaching the lens. See also **353**.

352 Improvised filters
Tape gelatin filters – bought as flexible sheets – in front of the lens of a simple camera if conventional filters are unavailable, or on any camera whose lens is not threaded to accept conventional filters.

353 Filter factors
Beware of confusing the meaning of filter factors. These concern anyone using a non-TTL camera, except automatics which have the meter sensor on the lens mount, so that the meter sensor is covered by the filter when in place.

Most filters absorb light (notable exceptions being skylight and ultraviolet) filters. The filter factor indicates the amount of extra exposure necessary to compensate. Manufacturers may give the factor either as a + or an × figure, usually shown on the filter case or mount. If the factor is, say, +2, it means give two stops more exposure. By contrast, ×2 means give double the exposure – in other words, open up one stop. A ×3 factor means open up $1\frac{1}{2}$ stops.

354 Skylight
Always (but see **356**) keep a skylight (or an ultraviolet) filter on your lens. It protects the front element and can cut down haze, reducing the bluish cast on colour film caused by ultraviolet radiation in the atmosphere. It is intended to be useful in the mountains or by the sea, where levels of scattered ultraviolet are high. The filter has a pale pink tint which may subtly warm colours. Many find however that its effect is barely noticeable.

355 UV
If you don't want the warming effect of a skylight filter (**354**), use an ultraviolet (UV) filter.

356
For preference, avoid using a skylight or UV with more than one other filter – loss of image quality builds up, especially with wide-angles.

357 Conversion filters
If you've loaded a daylight colour slide film, but want to shoot in tungsten light (as produced by photofloods or spotlights), use an 80A colour conversion filter. If the scene is lit by domestic bulbs, add an 82C.

358
There's no need for a conversion filter when using electronic flash or flash bulbs with daylight film.

359
To shoot tungsten light film in daylight or with flash, use an 85B (orange). Use an 82C for indoor shots lit by domestic bulbs.

360 Fluorescent light

Fluorescent tubes leave an unattractive greenish cast on colour film, and eliminating it needs special precautions. They can however be approximately corrected with an FL-D filter in conjunction with daylight film. Alternatively, bracket with CC10 magenta, CC20M and CC30M filters. The simplest solution, however, is to turn off the lights and use flash for illumination.

361 82 Series

Late afternoon and early evening light add warm tones to colour transparencies. If you don't want this effect, use one of the blue 82 series. But such correction is rarely necessary since most people find warm lighting enhances.

362 Creating mood

Use 80, 81, 82 and 85 series filters not just for their usual purpose of balancing or converting colour but to create or enhance mood. The 81 series are useful, for instance, for warming up the flat colours created by dull light.

363 Graduated filters

Blank skies can look boring, so use a graduated filter (either grey or blue, according to conditions) to fill in the empty area with subtle colour. Other colours are available for more dramatic effects, but make sure they harmonize with dominant colours in the scene. Graduated filters are also useful for reducing excessive contrast, for example in a bright sky dominating a sombre landscape. See also 364 and 365.

364

A grey graduated filter, with the grey part at the bottom of the frame, prevents unsightly overexposure of the foreground when using flash to light the middle distance.

365

Get the most subtle graduated effect from a graduated filter by using it with a telephoto lens at full aperture. The effect becomes more abrupt as you stop down, and especially so with a wide-angle lens.

366 Polarizing filters

To cut down reflection and glare from non-metallic objects like windows or water, use a polarizing filter. But remember it only works when shooting at an angle to the subject. You have to rotate the filter until the reflections are least evident. Doing this gradually decreases the intensity of light passing through the lens, so keep an eye on exposure. All polarizer effects vary with camera angle.

Without polarizing filter

With polarizing filter

367

Don't give up if you are caught without a conversion filter and want to expose colour print film in artificial light. A specialist processing laboratory can usually remove resulting casts very satisfactorily – with the exception of the greenish tinge made by fluorescent tubes. See also 67.

368

Don't use 81 and 82 series filters together – they cancel each other.

FILTERS

369
Don't overdo special filter effects: few photographic gimmicks can look so contrived.

370
Don't use your skylight or UV filter as the base for improvised soft-focus effects. Smearing anything on to the surface of a filter that ought to be regularly in use is inadvisable: and it might scratch in cleaning. Instead, use a plain sheet of glass held in front of the lens; alternatively buy a second skylight or UV just for the purpose.

371 Deeper blues
If you want to intensify – saturate – the colour of certain subjects, use a polarizing filter. Its effect on a brilliant blue sky is particularly impressive, but it will also improve other colours muted by high surface reflection, shiny foliage, for example, or the blue of a swimming pool. Remember you can also increase colour saturation by underexposing half a stop.

372 Combinations
You cannot only cut reflection but suffuse a scene with colour by using a colour polarizer. Combine it with a clear polarizer and you can increase colour saturation, too.

373 Soft focus
Achieve the romantic soft-focus effect reminiscent of vintage Hollywood movies by using soft focus filters. They work best at wide apertures (stopping down sharpens up any image) and if a subject has plenty of highlights – the bright spots are 'scattered', giving an extra-misty effect.

374 Breathing on the lens
If you do not possess a soft focus filter, try breathing on the lens. To make the condensation last longer, remove the lens from the camera and breathe on the rear element. Stretching a black stocking tightly over the lens gives a similar effect, and a coloured one can give an additional, delicate tint. Be prepared for substantial loss of image sharpness, and for best results experiment first. And remember, this softens the whole image. See also **373**.

375 Part soft focus
Small blobs or smears of an oily substance applied to a clear filter give selective diffusion: part will be misty, the rest sharp. Petroleum jelly is suitable for the purpose, and you can buy purpose-made gels, clear or coloured.

376 Diffraction
For spectrum-coloured flares and streaks across the image, try a diffraction filter. They work best with bright light sources in the picture.

377 Starburst
To maximize the effect of a starburst filter, use it with small, bright points of light such as street lamps in the picture, preferably against a dark background. Stop the lens well down and use the depth of field preview, if available, to judge the effect.

378 Multi-facet
Strong outlines against plain backgrounds give the best results with multi-facet filters, which are intended to produce multiple images.

379 Fog
Use fog filters separately or in multiple to get degrees of mistiness into landscape shots. They work by reducing contrast.

380 B/w or colour?
Use special effects filters such as polarizers, starbursts, soft focus and multi-faceted with black and white or colour. Use coloured filters – which are primarily designed to alter the way different tones record on black and white film – if you want special dramatic effects on colour film but remember they work best with subjects strongly outlined against plain backgrounds.

381 Yellow (with b/w)
Use it mainly for bringing out clouds in a blue sky, for recording foliage and flowers naturally or for accentuating the texture of sunlit snow. Darkens blue and lightens yellow.

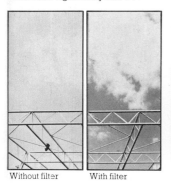

Without filter   With filter

382 Yellow-green (+b/w)
For natural skin tones in outdoor portraits, or contrast between sky and green landscapes; like yellow; reduces red.

383 Orange (with b/w)
Skies and open expanses of water significantly darkened; sunsets increased in contrast; texture of sunlit surfaces enhanced; distant haze reduced. Darkens blues and greens, reduces red.

384 Red (with b/w)
For dramatic increase in contrast in cloudy skies and stormy seas; spectacular sunsets. Use it with a polarizer to obtain 'day for night' (simulated moonlight). A deep red filter makes skies almost black. Lightens red and orange; darkens blues and greens.

385 Green (with b/w)
Useful in close-ups involving foliage – greens are lightened so enhancing detail. Suntans are deepened, but spotty, blotchy skin looks worse. Red or orange flowers show up strongly against their leaves. Darkens red and blue.

Without filter   With filter

386 Blue (with b/w)
For those rare occasions when you want to emphasize fog or haze. Lightens blues and purples, darkens yellows

387
Take care when using filter holders – as opposed to screw-in mounts – with wide-angle lenses. To be certain of the holder not intruding in the image, use a screw-in type with 24mm or wider lenses. Or use the large, square filters with larger-size holders designed for rollfilm cameras.

388
Don't rely on TTL meter readings when using deep-coloured filters such as a red or sepia. Take the meter reading without the filter in place, then open up by the recommended filter factor – see 353.

389
Don't use colour balancing and correcting filters with black and white film, on which they have little or no effect. They're designed for colour.

390
Don't carry around more equipment than you need. You'll soon regret loading yourself up with a heavy telephoto lens that you get no chance to use. Take only what you think you will really need. The items you will wish you had not left behind are usually small things such as filter adaptor rings, batteries or a cable release. If you keep them all together (an empty tobacco tin makes a good container) you'll always have them with you without adding much to your baggage.

391 Camera bags
Choose a bag that is slightly bigger than you think you need. If you cram everything into a bag that is too small you may damage delicate gear and you will find it difficult to get at small items, especially when you are in a rush. See **392** and **393**.

392 Plenty of pockets
Should you need to take extra equipment and don't want to carry a second bag wear an army jacket or a fisherman's waistcoat. You can distribute equipment among the pockets. Small items will tuck into tab pockets. Use large hip pockets for lenses (in cases), camera bodies and flash units. All will be readily accessible.

393 Adapting bags
If you use different combinations of equipment for particular types of assignment make your camera case or bag adaptable. Buy foam inserts and arrange them to suit different configurations of equipment. Have one for general use, one for camera bodies with telephoto lenses attached, one to carry flash or close-up equipment and others for a selection of lenses and bodies, according to your needs.

394 Checklist
If you do not use a carrying bag as the permanent home for your gear, make a checklist of all your equipment and tick off items as you load them up. Then you don't have to unpack the bag if you need to check whether you have remembered a particular item.

395 'Tool' bag
If you have a car, make full use of it as a base when you go out to take pictures. Pack a bag with those non-photographic accessories which you need surprisingly often, and keep it in the car. Such items include: clamps, pegs, pins and tape to hold things steady or in place; a silvered 'space blanket' to use as a reflector; a set of miniature screwdrivers (for tightening screws on camera and equipment); pliers, hammer, scissors, saw, knives; a bundle of clean, soft cloths; plugs and adaptors and a large plastic bag (dustbin liners are suitable) to put over both camera and tripod in a downpour; Swiss Army knife (see **861**).

Swiss Army knife

396 Memo holder
Many 35mm cameras have a memo holder mounted on the camera back, intended to hold the end of a film carton as an instant reminder of what film is loaded. The trouble with such holders is that they're usually too small to hold the carton end without cutting or tearing it; so for quick change-overs, keep a stock of trimmed carton ends in the equipment bag.

397 Neck-straps
If you're carrying two cameras around your neck, have one on a short strap and the other on a longer one. This makes it easier to change quickly from one to the other.

398
If carrying two cameras, one of which is fitted with a longer lens, that should hang on a longer neck-strap. If it's at chest level, it will get in the way when you change cameras.

399 Labelling
Keep handy a supply of adhesive-backed labels. They are useful for labelling film which you have up- or down-rated (**91** and **94**), for marking the number of exposures you have made on a film that is later to be reloaded, or for identifying film in a reusable cassette.

400 Theft and loss
Keep a detailed list of all your equipment, complete with its serial numbers. Make several copies of it, and all the relevant sales documents. Keep one set in your camera bag, one at home and one set in your workplace so that you are fully documented if it comes to reporting loss to police and insurance companies. Delays in reporting full details can prejudice claims and hinder chances of recovery.

401
Housebreakers like photographic goods. Reduce the risk of losing all your equipment to a thief by keeping it in a variety of places. A burglar may not bother to investigate an ordinary looking plastic shopping bag; but it could conceal a camera or lens suitably padded to disguise its shape.

402
Thieves know what camera bags look like. If you plaster your bag with trade stickers you are asking for trouble. Use an anonymous bag.

403 Insurance
Read the small print in your household policy. Check whether it offers replacement or only second-hand value, or requires costly items to be insured separately. If in doubt, ask your insurers.

404 Special policies
If you own what you consider to be a valuable collection of equipment, consider a policy aimed specifically at photographers. Premiums for professionals are high because of the increased risks they run, but for amateurs they can be reasonable. Not all policies give the same cover – for instance, not all cover equipment stolen from a locked car.

405
Don't carry an open camera bag in a crowd – you will risk something falling out and it will also act as a magnet for thieves. See also **402**.

406
Don't forget to make allowances for price increases and to add new equipment to your insurance policy when it comes up for renewal.

BEING PREPARED

407
Don't try to clean the mirror of a camera. Removing blemishes from its delicate coating is a specialist's job.

408
Don't waste time removing odd specks of dust – they won't affect the image, and persistent rubbing may damage lenses. Keep the inside of the camera scrupulously clean so that dust and grit don't scratch the film. Take care not to touch shutter blinds.

409
Don't use a cheap brush for cleaning: it will moult, adding to your problems. Use a fine artist's brush of good quality to coax dust from inaccessible areas.

410
Don't forget to depress the rewind button on a 35mm camera. Trying to drag the film back without doing so will tear through sprocket holes and possibly the film.

411 Cleaning
Keep lenses (both front and rear elements) and camera bodies clean. Remove dust and grit from the lens with a soft brush; start at the perimeter and sweep inwards in a spiral towards the centre, blowing dirt off with a blower brush or spray. Use lens tissue to *gently* rub off grease marks.

412 Batteries
Rub batteries and terminals from time to time with a clean cloth or a typewriter eraser to keep contacts clean. If one fails and no spare is available rub the contacts in this way. It may coax a few more minutes' life out of it.

413 Storage
Keep out-of-use equipment away from heat and moisture. Make use of silica-gel packs to absorb moisture.

414
Remove batteries from flash and motor-drive equipment to prevent leakage when they will be unused for a month or more.

415
Keep your camera's shutter speeds in trim by running through them all occasionally, since some are seldom used.

416 Film stocks
Keep unused film in a refrigerator. Allow time for it to warm up before use, never try to speed the process artificially. Film stored above 70°F (21°C) for more than four weeks may suffer changes in speed and colour balance. See also 49.

417
Keep a check on expiry dates of film stock, but see also **89**. If you have a quantity of outdated film, shoot off one roll first and check the results.

418 Loading film
Always load a camera in shade. If there is no shade turn your back to the sun and use your own shadow. If you have a camera with a shutter which won't operate in dull light, you may have to point it at a light source to advance the film.

419
Standardize your loading procedure. With 35mm film, make sure both lines of sprocket holes have been engaged and that the film leader is tucked firmly into the take-up spool.

420
Make it a habit to fire off the same number of blank frames at the start of a film. Should you wish to change films in mid-roll this will enable you to wind forward accurately when reloading partly shot film.

421 Winding on
Wind on always at the same time – either just before you take a picture, or immediately after. In this way you will always know whether the shutter has been tensioned or not – and so avoid trying to shoot when it is not. If you wish to bypass a camera's double exposure prevention system, see Assignment **8.** If you can't remember whether there is a film in the camera, try turning the rewind lever clockwise: if it resists, it's loaded.

SUBJECTS

A creative approach to individual subjects and situations
People • Special occasions • Sport • Nature • Wildlife • Pets
Landscape • Travel • Monuments • Close-up • Interiors
Still life • Extreme conditions

PEOPLE

422
Don't photograph people with bright sun in their eyes. See **427–428, 229** and **240–241**.

423
Don't include so much background that attention is drawn away from the subject.

424
Don't fiddle with the camera controls in a portrait-sitter's presence, and especially not if trying to take a picture unobserved.

425
Don't disappoint sitters by shooting them when not looking their best. You almost always get a more patient sitter if you allow him or her to prepare.

426 Remember
Most photographs of people are spoilt by their being too far from the camera. See **206–207.**

427
Resist the inclination to shoot people in bright sunlight. You almost always get a better picture if you move them to the shade. Modern negative films (i.e. for prints) have the tolerance to incorrect exposure to give acceptable results in light shade even if the camera offers no exposure adjustment.

428 Hat on
If there's no shade, try making the subject wear a wide-brimmed hat. Make sure the shadow covers the whole face. See **427.**

429 Flash
You can reduce ugly shadows and heavy contrast with direct or fill-in flash – see **286–289.**

430 How close?
As a rule, move in close enough to fit head plus shoulders into the frame, but also check whether the picture could have extra impact if you cropped in close to the hairline. The face is, after all, the most interesting feature. If using a non-reflex camera at close range, see **211.**

431 Full-length
If a full-length shot takes your fancy, fine – but think before shooting whether there's good reason for this approach: will it show off the subject's clothes, for instance, or some activity they're engaged in?

432 Always
Keep backgrounds simple. They should be *part* of the composition – not just backdrops. Use a doorway or arch as a frame; make your subject look out at you through a window.

433 Props
Hands usually look awkward. Give your subject something to hold – perhaps an object that reflects their personality or interests – flowers, a musical instrument, some item of sports equipment.

434
If you can't find something for a sitter to hold, get a man to put his hands in his pockets, a woman to clasp them in front.

435 Absorbed
If you have the chance, photograph family or friends when absorbed in activities they enjoy – garden, hobbies, even cleaning the car. Such shots reflect personality and minimize self-consciousness.

436 Family and friends

If you can avoid wheeling family or friends out into the open for a formal, posed group, do so. Instead, shoot them engaged in some common activity, like having a meal or playing a game: this emphasizes bonds.

437 Group backgrounds

Look for suitable group backgrounds in advance, so you can organize the subjects quickly, without making anyone impatient. Simple backgrounds are best: a tree, an open doorway, a flight of steps.

438 Ideas

Try looking at record sleeves for original ideas on posing groups and for suitable backgrounds: witness the range of ideas just in the shots below.

439 Focus

Arrange groups so there's an obvious focal point of the gathering – the oldest relative, the new baby, the birthday girl. Gain impact by placing the star' in the foreground and shoot with a wide-angle.

440 Cohesion

Have groups bunch really close – it adds a surprising amount of intimacy.

441 Insurance

Not everyone in a group will smile at once. Take two or three shots to improve your chances. It's impossible to keep an eye on them all at the same time, so aim for a sprinkling of interesting expressions and/or smiles.

442

Don't pose groups in huddles in the middle of nowhere. The shot's always more interesting if the location is relevant – but see 439.

443

Don't attempt an unrepeatable, formal group portrait without the camera mounted on a tripod or suitable support. It lets you frame the shot, then walk up to the group to make vital adjustments. Use a long cable release and you can shoot them unawares; with you behind the camera, they're more likely to appear self-conscious.

FACIAL FEATURES

444
Watch for reflections in glasses, especially if using flash. Test-fire to judge the effect.

445
Don't shoot someone who has double chins from below, or with the head angled downwards – the feature will be emphasized.

446
Don't shoot bony, angular faces in hard, direct lighting, or strong side-lighting – both will emphasize such features and create deep shadows.

447 Glasses
Make sure the tops of the frames don't cut across the subject's eyes. Move the glasses slightly, or change position.

448 Long nose
If your subject has a long, angular nose, shoot from just below the line of the mouth and keep the face square-on to the camera. If you can, use a short telephoto – **311** – or a teleconverter – see **340–348**.

449
Mask prominent ears by having the subject turn the head so that one ear is hidden. Then light the subject so the other ear is in shadow.

450 Wrinkles
Hide wrinkles by using soft, diffused light and/or a soft focus attachment (**373–375**).

451 Deep sockets
If your subject has deep-set eyes and heavy brows, use a diffused light at eye-level and shoot from a low angle – this ought to prevent the sockets coming out as black holes.

452 Expressive eyes
To emphasize these, have the head tilted downwards and the eyes looking up.

453 Broad face
Make a face look narrower by shooting from a high angle and making the subject look away from the camera.

454 Weak chin
Strengthen chins by shooting upwards from a low angle.

455 Authority
Suggest this by shooting from a low angle.

456 Graceful neck
Have the sitter look upwards to emphasize the neck.

457 Wrinkled neck
Ensure the head is level, and/or ask the sitter to look downwards. Light from above so the neck area is in shadow.

458 Not much hair
Disguise thinning hair by shooting from below. Light from the side at face level.

459 Emphasizing hair
Do this with backlighting.

460 Double chin
Shoot from eye level or above, and have the subject look upwards so the jaw juts out.

461 Improvement
If you seriously want to take good photographs of people, keep an eye out for any pictures that please you. With each one, ask yourself why you like it. The common element will almost certainly be (a) the sitter looks good and (b) the shot tells you something of their character

462 Which way to look?
As a rule, it's best to ask sitters to look at you; and if you want the most direct eye-contact of all, ask them to look into the lens.

463 Sharp eyes
Always focus on the eyes in a portrait. They are the most expressive feature and if they aren't sharp, impact is lost.

464 Angle-to-camera
Most people photograph best with head and/or shoulders at an angle to the camera.

465 Character
Suggest a strong personality by having the sitter lean forwards towards the camera.

466 Side views
Emphasize a strong profile by having the subject look up with the head tilted back.

467 Pensive look
For this expression, or for a relaxed or submissive look, ask the subject to lean back and slightly bow the head.

468 Star quality
To achieve the glamorous, haughty look, ask the sitter to face you almost full-on, then turn the head sideways and slightly upwards, looking out of the frame.

469 Come-on
An over-the-shoulder glance can be suggestive, but beware of wrinkles showing up at the back of the neck. If you can't eliminate them by turning the head to and fro, disguise them with a scarf.

470 Guile
Often the best shot is taken at the moment a person relaxes – and this is more often than not the moment after you've taken a shot. So pretend to shoot, or waste a couple of frames – and then take your chance at the critical moment.

471 Patter
Have a stock of amusing stories to tell, and anticipate not only the smiles and laughter but the way the eyes open expressively just before the punchline.

472
Try getting the sitter to talk, or tell a story to the lens.

473
For a serious look, ask the sitter's views on some weighty topic of the day.

474
Beware of the face-on, head-and-shoulders shot. Unless it's of an unusually spontaneous expression, it tends to look like a police 'mug shot'.

475
Don't photograph less-than-attractive chins and noses in profile, it only emphasizes them.

476
Don't try to coax a smile out of someone who's the serious type. It will probably look forced, and photographing them naturally is more likely to reveal their personality.

CANDID

477
Don't spend a long time with the camera to your eye – people notice. Frame the picture mentally, preset the controls and look through the viewfinder only at the last moment.

478
Avoid candid shots, however interesting they seem at the time, where the subject's face isn't in the shot. Surprising numbers of candid shots are spoilt because of backs, or sides, turned to the camera.

479 Remember
The golden rule of candid photography is not entirely obvious: take your time. It's not enough just to steal any shot of an unaware subject. People look surprisingly wooden and awkward if shot simply as they go about their business. So wait for the moments that stand out – the animated gesture, a quick smile or burst of laughter, the frown of concentration.

480 Stealth
The obvious way of remaining unnoticed is to shoot from a distance with a telephoto lens; but approaching your subject from an unexpected angle can be equally effective.

Choice of telephoto tends to be dictated by circumstance, but the shorter focal lengths – 85 to 150mm – are useful.

481 Preparation
There may not be time to focus accurately, so preset the focus by estimating distance and choose as narrow an aperture as possible to give sufficient depth of field. Take a meter reading from an object similar to your subject (your hand?) and preset the exposure controls. Use a fast shutter speed if possible – working quickly to avoid being observed adds to the chances of camera shake.

482 Wide-angle candid
If you can get close to your subject without causing selfconsciousness, try shooting with a wide-angle. These lenses give a strong sense of immediacy and involvement which is much in the spirit of candid photography.

483
Exploit the wide-angle's generous depth of field by shooting from the hip, without bringing the camera to the eye. Point the camera casually in the general direction of your subject and fire when you will. All controls need to be preset, but don't worry about accurate framing – crop or mask the image at the processing stage. Autofocus compacts are ideal for this technique.

484 Composition
Strong expressions and interesting gestures will carry many a candid shot, but it's worth doing everything possible to eliminate clashing colours and fussy, unsightly backgrounds. Just snapping a fleeting moment isn't enough for the outstanding candid picture; compose as carefully as you would for any other shot.

485 Lighting
Diffused, soft lighting is almost essential for babies' rounded features. Often you can't do better than load a fast film and shoot by available light near a window.

486 First picture
The transparent plastic cribs in use at many hospitals are ideal for the first shots of a baby, who can lie there undisturbed while you shoot, the face evenly lit right down to mattress level. Load a fast film.

487 Props
Rather than photograph babies lying in their prams (where lighting is difficult) or being held (when hands intrude), prop them up in a chair on cushions; but see **499.**

488
From about six weeks, babies are interested in mobiles; exploit this to get shots of facial expressions. Blank babies' faces are boring.

489 Not to be missed
Photograph all the main events in a baby's day – feeding, bathing, sleep and play – commonplace now, but not later.

490 Angle
Get down to their level: it gives the pictures immediacy.

491 Amusement
Give a child a toy to play with – preferably brightly coloured.

492 Resourcefulness
Producing a surprise toy halfway through a session can stave off boredom for a few more minutes. Try bubble-blowing: it gives interesting facial expressions and the bubbles themselves look good if well lit.

493
With toddlers and younger children, ask the mother to be present. She will be better than you at making them react, and their relationship comes across well in photographs.

494
There's no point in trying to make children stay still and pose for long periods when you can get most of the best shots – formal and informal – by following them around. Preset the camera (see **183**) and if you own a zoom, use it.

495 Opportunities
Tears and tantrums are photogenic – shoot them if you can.

496
Try putting a child in the driver's seat of a car and telling him he's a racing driver.

497 Participation
Involve children in photography: they'll enjoy 'helping'.

498
Don't ask children to tolerate more than about ten minutes' concentrated, posed picture-taking. Freshness is everything with child photography. See also **494.**

499
Beware of placing babies or children against or near strongly coloured objects, including grass when shooting in colour. Colour casts can be reflected into the face, and the result can be ugly.

500
Don't risk running out of film. You will shoot much more film than you expect when covering any occasion or ceremony. Estimate how much you think you will need by referring to a rough 'shooting script' – see **506** – then double the quantity.

501
Don't try to do everything yourself. Whenever a ceremony or occasion requires group shots, get an assistant to help organize people into position while you concentrate on operating the camera.

502
Don't try to take pictures of the bride leaving home for the ceremony. You need to be quickly away in order to get the vital shots of her arriving at the church, synagogue or place where the ceremony is to be conducted.

503 Preparation
Check equipment thoroughly some days beforehand (in time to get repairs done if necessary) and again on the actual day. Take spare batteries. See 390–399.

504 Location check
Visit the location beforehand: check out camera positions, vantage points, backgrounds.

505 Commissions
If you are taking pictures for someone else, ask what they most want recorded.

506 Shooting script
For any special occasion, make a plan of the shots you want, scene by scene. For a wedding it might run: 1 Bride preparing at home. 2 Arrival of groom and best man where the ceremony is to take place. 3 Bride and father (or whoever is to give her away) arriving at the ceremony. 4 Exchanging vows. 5 Exchanging rings. 6 Formal groups after the ceremony. 7 Confetti. 8 Greeting reception guests. 9 The bride's attend-

ants, if she has any. 10 The groom and best man, plus any other supporters. 11 Speeches. 12 Cutting the cake. 13 Leaving.

507 Crowds
There is usually a crush to see the bride and groom leaving the church, synagogue or ceremony. Make sure you are at the front; fit a wide-angle lens to get the couple in at close quarters.

508 Over their heads
If practical, use a step ladder to raise yourself above the crowd. If you have an alloy equipment case, try standing on that.

509 Film choice
Commercial wedding photographers usually use rollfilm cameras, whose negative size gives better enlargements than 35mm. Consider borrowing or hiring such a camera for shooting a wedding and, if you do, practise with it before the day. If shooting with 35mm, load a slow (100 ISO) film – the fine grain will enhance enlargements. Take fast film, too, for indoors and poor light.

510 Formal pictures
Study professional wedding shots and note especially how they place people in relation to the camera, position hands and feet, arrange veils and trains.

511 Who's who
Make sure you recognize the bride and all principal relations of the bride and groom.

512 Arrivals
If the wedding ceremony takes place in a building with fine doors or porches – be it church, synagogue, temple, town hall or registry office – shoot the newly arrived bride and whoever gives her away framed in a doorway or porch.

513 Nerves
Guests arriving at ceremonies are often slightly selfconscious. Better photograph them later when more relaxed.

514 High angle
Exploit the gallery or upper level in a church or other religious building to get shots of the bride and groom before the altar and walking out.

515
Shooting from above may help cram extra people into a group picture, and add interest.

516 Frames
Look out for attractive settings in which to photograph the bride, especially ones which form a natural frame.

517 Line-ups
Choose a neat, tidy setting for all your posed shots. Keep groups square on to the background. Choose neutral-coloured backgrounds.

518 Greetings
Shoot as many frames as you can of the couple receiving their guests – in this way you are most likely to achieve at least one shot in which everyone looks animated.

519
Take reception photographs before tables get cluttered.

520 Cake cutting
Mask table debris with flowers, and tell the couple to look up.

521 The bridal portraits
Photograph her standing alone with her head half-turned towards the camera, looking at the lens. Take shots of the couple looking at each other.

522
Try to photograph the couple away from their guests for a while in a more relaxed atmosphere so that they can be themselves.

523 Going away
Make sure that you leave the reception before the couple so that you are in position to photograph their departure. Take several frames of them driving down the road to make a natural ending to the set.

524
Don't let car doors obscure the bride and groom. Shoot from the open side, or use a high angle.

525
Don't start taking impromptu shots at any stage of a wedding until you have all the 'standard' shots required of each stage of the proceedings. The hosts, and the couple, want to remember every stage of the day by its pictures – because for them, the day tends to be a confused whirl.

ACTION/SPORT

526
Don't attempt to follow everything that happens at a sporting event. Concentrate on a player or competitor you think has potential; you are far more likely to achieve results.

527 Remember
A fast film – 400 or 1000 ISO – enables you to use fast shutter speeds in poor lighting. See **64** and **83**.

528 Stadium sports
Get close enough to the action for it to dominate the shot. If you have only a standard or short telephoto this may mean restricting yourself to play close to your position. Shots of action the other side of the ground rarely work. A zoom lens is ideal for this type of photography – see **330**.

529 Off duty
Players' off-guard moments, when they are not involved in play, make good pictures.

530 Backgrounds
Keep an eye on backgrounds. A packed crowd adds atmosphere, but beware of such clutter as advertising signs, floodlights, groundsmen's equipment and concession stalls. These can be a special problem if using a wide-angle.

531 Crowds
Watch the crowd as well as the game. An individual's joy or despair can make a good candid subject.

532 Tight composition
Try to shoot when players or competitors are bunched up together. If they are stretched out across the field, or along a track, the sense of urgency is lost. A telephoto creates bunching along the lens's axis.

533 Monopod
In confined conditions, such as stadium seating, where a tripod would take up too much room, try using a monopod.

534 Ball games
Shoot just after the player has made contact with the ball. The face will be at its most expressive. Always aim to include the ball. See Assignment **5**.

535 Prefocus
In races or other events when you can predict the position of your subject, focus in advance (see 198).

536 Electronic flash
This is invaluable for freezing movement within its range.

537 Uprating film
Uprating your film (see 91) may be the only way of using a long lens with a relatively narrow maximum aperture at a shutter speed fast enough for action pictures. The resulting grain, contrary to spoiling the result, can add greatly to its effect, especially for a tough game played in far-from-ideal weather conditions.

538 Floodlighting
If an event is being televised you can make use of the additional lighting. TV floods are usually daylight-balanced.

539 Unknown light type
If you want to shoot colour, but are unsure about what kind of lighting is in use in the stadium, use colour negative film and filter out any casts when making prints. See 67.

540 Panning
Capitalize on this technique (219) for sporting subjects. It will help you to get a strong action picture, even in poor light or with a fixed-speed camera. Use it like selective focusing (178) to reduce unsightly background to a uniform blur, and adding to the impression of speed. Combine panning with zooming (336) for interesting effects.

541 Camera angle
Emphasize action by the angle of the shot. Low for a jumper, for example.

542 Motor drives
Automatic winders and motor drives are useful for action photography because you don't have to take your eye from the viewfinder between shots, and film transport is much faster than by the usual method. However, these devices offer no guarantee of securing dramatic action shots – despite the amount of film used. If a motor drive can fire three frames per second, and the shutter is set to 1/500, you will only ever capture 3/500 of the action on film each second. The other 497/500 will be devoted to film transport and other mechanical functions. See also 859, 862 and 863.

543 Anticipation
The drawbacks of motor drives and power winds should make it clear that there's no substitute for anticipating the climactic moment that makes a great action shot.

544
Don't waste energy getting 'authentic' action shots when they can be faked. You can't re-run a horse race, but there are many events which can be re-staged during non-competitive practice. If you want a set of pictures of the local football team, it may be much more rewarding to shoot them in training.

545
Don't be a loner at popular sporting events. Look out for where the press photographers have positioned themselves and try to get near. They know the best picture-taking locations from experience.

546
Don't photograph imperfect specimens – a small blemish easily goes unnoticed when you're busy with setting up a shot, but is all too noticeable in the final result.

547
Avoid shooting trees close-to with a wide-angle or standard lens. You'll be forced to tilt the camera upwards to frame the top of the tree; and this gives converging verticals, which make trees look as if they are falling over backwards. The solution is to change to a telephoto and shoot from a distance.

548 Remember
The shape, form, texture or colour of some relatively small part of a plant or flower can be as interesting as the whole.

549
Take advantage of the static nature of plant subjects to explore lighting angles at leisure. Many flowers look best backlit, the translucent quality of petals adding an extra ingredient to the picture. Strongly textured leaves are shown best by side-lighting..

550
Try different viewpoints; get down to the level of the plant. Shooting from above can however emphasize symmetry.

551 Depth of field
The zone of sharp focus (see **172**) is dramatically reduced in close-up work. Turn this to advantage by taking single blooms sharply focused against a wash of blurred background colour. Remember, however, that a single part of a flower or plant, with the rest out of focus, is rarely effective. To achieve the narrow apertures vital for reasonable, working depth of field, you'll have to use slow shutter speeds and fast film; both have drawbacks – see **553** and **64**. Consider using flash – see **286–290** and **718**.

552 Backgrounds
If a background is distracting, or the wrong colour for the subject, have a companion stand so that their shadow falls behind the subject. Or shoot upwards against the sky. If the camera is automatic, and has an exposure locking mechanism, lock in correct exposure beforehand. See also **725**.

553 Windshield
Plants moving in the breeze present a major problem: to freeze the motion, you need a fast shutter speed; to achieve depth of field (see **172**) you usually need a slow speed. The standard solution is a simple, fabric windshield, mounted on poles driven into the ground. White fabric doubles as a reflector. See also Assignment **6** and tip **717**.

554 Preparation
Find out about the habits of the animals or birds you want to photograph. Knowing when and where to look is essential.

555 Being unobtrusive
Approach slowly at an even pace, with frequent stops, during which you should 'freeze'. If the animal or bird seems unconcerned, try a few steps further. If possible, stoop or crawl: creatures find an upright approach threatening.

556 Scent
If possible, approach downwind of the animal.

557 Glitter
Mask shiny surfaces on equipment with black tape.

558 Camera locations
Careful study of an area, preferably with a local expert, will reveal the best places to set up a camera. Some animals – for example deer – will return regularly to an open clearing where the feed is good; even more willingly if a lump of hard salt is put down for them to lick.

559 Hides
Once you know the best camera location, think of constructing a simple hide – unless the natural cover is good enough in itself. Some of the simplest and best hides are made of natural materials.

560 Artificial hides
Among professional wildlife photographers, the trend is towards the simplest possible

hides. If the terrain dictates a man-made hide, keep it simple, and improvise: camouflage pattern cloth draped over three or four stakes in the ground can work well; as can an ordinary camper's tent, provided it is a dull colour.

561 Car-hide
A stationary car with the engine switched off can be as good a hide as any, offering ideal picture-taking opportunities of, amongst other creatures, the smaller (and tamer) woodland birds. Simply stop in a woodland car parking area, or pull up on the roadside. Open the window and rest the camera on a bean bag.

562 Deception
Animals don't count. If two people enter a hide, then one leaves soon afterwards, the creature(s) will assume the hide is now empty. But don't expect fast results.

563 Super-patient
Even when a creature finally appears, wait until it settles into the location. It is less likely to be disturbed by camera noise if, for instance, it is busy eating.

564 Mirror noise
If using an SLR camera on a tripod, and the camera offers the facility of manually raising the mirror, use it: camera noise will be much reduced.

565
Don't wear bright colours when photographing animals. Preferably wear a dull green that will merge with background. A hat pulled well down over the face may help – many animals and birds seem to automatically take alarm at the pale, round shape of the human face.

566
Don't go out photographing wildlife without first checking that local conservation codes permit it. In many countries there are severe penalties, for example on anyone disturbing protected birds at their nests.

ZOOS/RESERVES/PETS

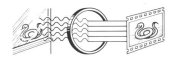

567
Don't get so excited at your first sight of big game that you fire away indiscriminately – the results will be disappointing.

568
Don't take yet another picture of sleeping lions. Wait until you can catch some action. Even if it is only a yawn, or the head being raised, it will make all the difference.

569 Zoos
If a net fence stands in the way, go close to it and shoot with as wide an aperture as possible. The effect of depth of field (**172**) will render it invisible if the camera is focused on an animal in the middle or far distance. The effect is magnified with a telephoto lens.

570 Glass
If you have to shoot through glass, minimize dirt and distortion by putting the camera lens right up to it. Use depth of field (**172**) to keep it well out of focus. A lens hood, or a suitably cupped hand, cuts out reflection, as does a polarizing filter – see **366** and **371–372**.

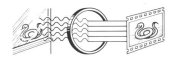

571 Safari parks
When car windows have to be kept closed, go ahead and shoot through them, but clean them thoroughly first. If the car is moving, hold the lens near the glass, not against it, otherwise car movement and vibration will create camera shake. Shooting through glass, provided the right technique (**570**) is used, rarely spoils a picture.

572 Nature reserves
Most reserves have hides set up especially for visitors. Find out about them in advance by calling the reserve management. Ask what is to be seen and at what distance. It may be worth hiring special equipment – for example a super telephoto lens.

573 Big game
Driving along dirt roads kicks up dust. On safari, keep equipment in plastic bags or dust-proof containers. See **740**.

574
Big cats tend to congregate in the same place every day, often at first light or in the very early morning. Sometimes wardens or rangers put down food to attract the animals. Other types of animal gather at waterholes. Get your 'guaranteed' shots from such locations as a priority; they may be your only chances of good pictures.

575 Pets
An assistant is invaluable for photographing domestic animals. Ask them to attract the animal's attention (if necessary with food); this often opens up a good profile shot. And get the assistant to restrain the pet from investigating the camera at close quarters.

576
Pets interrelating with or being shown off by their owners have a double level of interest.

577 Table-top studio
Place smaller pets on a table top: convenient for shooting at their level.

578 Dogs
Expect more trouble photographing small dogs than larger dogs; the latter are less restless. Plan accordingly; most dogs are least restless after feeding.

579 Action
If a dog has any retriever instinct – and many breeds do – probably the easiest way to capture a lively action shot is to throw a stick or ball in the air and shoot as the animal leaps to catch it.

580 Cats
If you find it hard to photograph domestic cats you are not alone – some professional photographers think them the most difficult of all subjects. Try putting a cat on a sheet of glass – it often has a temporary freezing effect.

581
A cat often has a regular place where it sits to wash or to look out through a window. Prefocus on the spot – 198 – and wait.

582
You can often get a good full-body shot of a cat by noting a stretch of fence it often walks along. Prefocus on a specific point, set a suitable shutter speed (see 214–218) and let the cat walk into the frame.

583 Aquarium fish
The major problem with fish in a tank is keeping them in a zone of sharp focus. Try restricting their movement by lowering a sheet of glass into the tank, parallel with the side from which you want to photograph. It won't show up in the final result.

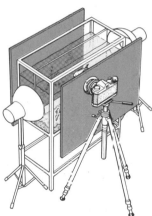

584
Don't shoot straight down at an animal lying by your feet. It's almost bound to look boring. Get down to the animal's level and try several viewpoints.

585
Don't photograph pets without checking for dirty specks in the eyes and ears. You may not notice them in the viewfinder, but you will on the processed picture.

LANDSCAPE

586
Don't place the horizon through the exact centre of the frame – it looks wrong. If the sky is the most dramatic element of the picture, let it dominate. If the ground is more important, exclude most or all of the sky. If in doubt as to where exactly the horizon should lie, mentally divide the frame into three horizontal, equal parts. The horizon, or any strong horizontal line, should lie either a third from the top or the bottom.

587
Watch out for foreground clutter – cars, roads, fences, tourists – when photographing views: frame them out unless they help the composition.

588 Equipment
Choose your lens according to the statement you want to make about the landscape.

589
A wide-angle lens will probably be best if you want to emphasize its sweep; and, of course, if you require plenty of depth of field.

590
To express the grandeur and dominance of the scenery use a telephoto lens to compress the perspective.

591
A standard lens will help you to set detail against the whole without distortion.

592
Atmospheric haze requires special precautions – see **732** and **735–736**.

593
Use a slow film to record fine detail, but remember grainy (fast) film can add atmosphere to the scene and, especially if pushed (see **92–93**), can give a *pointilliste* effect.

594 Format
Use the horizontal ('landscape') format to convey the expanse of a landscape; use the vertical ('portrait') one to express its strength. Cropping prints to a panoramic format (3:1) suits sweeping views.

595 Composition
Employ lead-in lines to draw the eye through the picture.

596
Produce a feeling of depth by making use of graphic and perspective effects in the lie of the land such as the zigzag of a valley or the overlapping lines of receding hills.

597 Long-distance shots
Photograph popular tourist spots from a distance in order to cut out intrusive cars, signs, concession stalls and people. Soft focus foreground detail can block eyesores, adding colour and depth.

598 Scale
Try to suggest the scale of landscape – a tiny figure or cottage in the middle of a huge expanse is often enough to convey this vital element.

599 High viewpoints
It's worth the effort of walking up hills for landscape shots. The high viewpoint rarely fails to provide a fresh perspective, and will often help you cut out unwanted foreground detail.

600 Lighting
Shoot in all types of light, and see **231** to **246**. Unsettled weather will give many more interesting landscape opportunities than all-day sun, but be prepared to manipulate film (see **90–96**) processing to enhance the atmosphere of a sombre, rainy day. If shooting in colour, don't miss out on the dramatic contrast created by weak sunlight illuminating a scene dominated by dark storm clouds.

601 Choice conditions
The most interesting lighting is usually early and late in the day – see **238–239** and **241–242**.

602 Famous views
Some views are too famous not to photograph; but the thought of duplicating hundreds of other postcards and snaps is depressing. In this situation, try shooting into the light. It reduces modelling and detail but emphasizes a familiar shape by putting it into total or partial silhouette

603 Foreground detail
Try shooting very low with a wide angle lens, including some foreground detail that appeals – perhaps a flower, a fallen tree or a boat. It leads the eye into the landscape and if the foreground detail is well chosen, can suggest your own interpretation of the scene.

604
Don't ignore colours in landscape, even if you're shooting in black and white. Think how they will render in grey tones, and consider using filters to bring them out – **381** to **386**.

605
Don't shoot views from a moving vehicle if there are trees or telegraph poles along the way. It is practically impossible to prevent them intruding in the shot, and they usually record as blurs because of their closeness to the camera.

606 Exposure
The recurring problem of landscape photography is how to expose correctly when there is a large, bright expanse of sky. See **153**. Consider using a graduated filter (**363–365**) with colour or black and white. With black and white, consider using a filter to emphasize cloud detail – **381**.

Graduated filter

607 The sun
Make use of the sun as a dramatic picture element. Actually included in the frame, it can convey varying mood, from the heat of noon to the tranquillity of the end of the day. To prevent the disc burning out you have to slightly underexpose the land; take an average reading from the horizon if you want to record as much land detail as possible.

608 Water
Large expanses of water can be visually boring. Build in some foreground elements or give prominence to the sky.

609
To add sparkle to water, shoot into the light. Even if a river is only a minor element in the shot, it will draw the eye if it catches the light.

610
Use a slow speed on a tripod-mounted camera to suggest the flow of water. It will look misty while objects around appear sharp. Try the effects of different speeds slower than 1/15 – they will vary according to water's speed of flow.

611 Details
A close shot of a carefully chosen detail – perhaps the furrows in a field or the patterns in a sand dune – can suggest the essence of both landscapes and general views.

612 Colour

Look for patches of colour – however small – and use them as focal points for landscape shots. You can introduce it 'artificially' by asking a companion to put on a brightly coloured item of clothing; harmonious colours are usually most effective.

613 Aerial photography

Going up in a plane, large or small, presents exciting picture opportunities, but results can be disappointing. Before shooting, ask yourself whether haze is going to eliminate all punch from the final result. Sometimes it cannot be eliminated, even if you take the usual precautions – see **354–355**. Then, be highly selective. The view from above which seemed fascinating at the time is all too often flat and boring in a photograph because the light,' from directly overhead, showed up no relief. Unless the sun is from near the horizon, be ultra-selective in what you shoot, making up for flatness with shots that single out interesting shapes and patterns on the ground.

614

Cloud formations shot from above usually work well.

615

Reflections in windows of pressurized aircraft cause special problems. The double glazing gives two reflective surfaces, and can set up weird multi-coloured effects. Polarizing filters are only partially effective. Cupping a hand round the lens, or fitting a lens hood, is usually the most effective course. See **570** for correct procedure when photographing through glass.

616 Urban landscape

Towns and cities offer landscape photography just like the countryside. Echo the rolling of hills in the successive rows of rooftops, or use a long lens to bunch up groups of tall buildings as if they were a range of peaks. Get effective shots by emphasizing the linear perspective of streets.

617

If you can find the right vantage point, shoot a whole sweep of urban landscape at dusk, just as the lights come on. Expose to give maximum detail in the unlit areas, and let the lights burn out. Include any rich colour in the evening sky.

618

Be alert to details above your head, and at ground level when you walk about a town or city. The upper parts of older buildings usually carry fascinating architectural details. The heavy texture of cobblestones, the pattern of light on steps, even manhole covers may offer picture opportunities.

619
Don't make a big display of your equipment when abroad. The photographer who goes about bristling with cameras and lenses can be the object of resentment and mistrust, particularly in poorer countries. He, or she, is also a target for theft and even violence. Leave big telephotos at home or put them in your case if walking round a crowded market.

620
Don't leave cameras, film or other equipment lying in sunlight. See 416 and 750.

621
Don't be lulled into thinking your hotel room is secure from theft, even if you lock it up. In hot countries, gaps are sometimes left in walls for ventilation, and bold thieves will fish for goods even if you are asleep in the room. To be safe, lock gear in a cupboard, or take a locking camera case and padlock it to the plumbing. See also 400–406.

622 Packing
When you pack your bags to go abroad, try to imagine what the photographic conditions in your destination will be like and choose your equipment accordingly. A polarizing filter, for instance, can be invaluable in the tropics for darkening blue skies. On an autumn trip to Ireland and its mists, however, you could well be lost without an 81 series warming filter. And on a skiing trip, it is well worth taking a compact 35mm camera to carry around on the slopes instead of bulky and vulnerable SLR equipment.

623 Where to buy film?
You can get film in nearly every country in the world nowadays, but it is still better to take all your films with you. If you buy ten or more films, you can often get bulk discount, and at home you can be sure of getting exactly the right film, stored in the right conditions.

624 Spares
Take spare batteries for camera and flashgun – see 412.

625 Humidity
If you are to travel in damp or humid climates, see 413.

626 Air travel
It is best to take photographic equipment as hand baggage on the plane to minimize risk of damage through careless handling. Only items like tripods should go in the aircraft's hold; ideal for carrying a tripod is a golf club bag – and some airlines carry golf clubs free of charge.

627 X-rays and film
If you and your films have passed through airport X-ray detector machines more than four times on a trip, put the films in a transparent plastic bag and ask for them to be examined by hand. Exposure to certain levels of X-rays has the same effect on film as exposure to light, and fast colour films are particularly sensitive to X-rays. With the older type of X-ray machine still used outside Europe and the US, even a single dose can be enough to ruin a film. You can buy special lead foil bags to protect film, but they are not always effective because the machine operator often turns up the power to see what may be in the package.

Fogged by X-rays

628 Map
Buy a map of the area if you plan to stay some time; it may reveal some new and interesting viewpoint for a popular landmark and perhaps some fascinating places you would not otherwise have photographed at all. A map that shows relief is particularly useful if you are looking for high vantage points for arresting landscape shots.

629 Off the beaten track

Be prepared to explore places away from the tourist centres. You are far more likely to find genuine local colour and the experience of discovery could well inspire you to take better pictures.

630 Photo essay

If you want, you can shoot exactly the same type of pictures on your travels as at home; but the real challenge is to sum up places photographically. Set yourself the task of creating a photo essay or documentary showing the distinctive nature of people, landscape and climate. This approach almost guarantees at least a few interesting, non-stereotyped shots.

631 Postcard art

When you first arrive in a new place, make a quick tour of the postcard shops. Postcards reveal the famous local sights and some ways of photographing them – plus some ways not to photograph them.

632 Markets

If you are after shots that capture the flavour of a place, few locations are better than the market place. The combination of bustling activity and natural light makes market places ideal for candids. The colourful local produce provides useful backgrounds, or fascinating subjects in their own right. Go out of your way to visit local, not tourist markets.

633 The bad and the ugly

If you want a realistic, balanced impression, find and take pictures of the less attractive aspects of a place as well as the obvious beauty spots.

634

Don't come home with a succession of 'views' and nothing else. However inspiring they were at the time, you'll be disappoined with results if they aren't mixed with pictures that have the obvious types of impact: close-ups of friends or family in unusual settings, candids of local people going about their business, shots of local landmarks. Views are difficult to take well – see **586–618**.

MONUMENTS

635
Beware of telegraph wires and other distractions in the foreground when photographing monuments or great buildings. Look at the view without the camera as well as scanning the viewfinder carefully – telegraph wires are virtually invisible in the viewfinder but they will be obtrusive in a photograph. If you cannot avoid shooting through telegraph wires, use a wide aperture to keep them out of focus (see **178**) or try to arrange the shot so they cross in front of a dark part of the monument or building. See also **640** and **641**.

636 New shots for old
Nearly every major monument or building in the world, from the Taj Mahal to the Statue of Liberty, has been photographed countless times. Yet most travellers shoot from the same old viewpoints and end up with almost identical pictures. If you want something a little more interesting, walk around the monument and study it from different angles.

637 Eye for detail
Move in close on interesting details – see **618**. With large-scale buildings, a telephoto is essential for closing in on details far above.

638
If there are fine mouldings or relief work on a building or monument, preferably shoot early in the morning or in the evening when the sun is at a low angle, lighting the surface from the side. This brings out texture and relief.

639 Walk away
Finding a new and interesting view of a monument may be as simple as walking down a side street. You may not get a clear view of the subject, but it could be interesting to show how the monument looms over buildings in its vicinity.

640 Vantage point
If the foreground seems cluttered, one solution is to find a high vantage point (**599**). In built-up areas this may not be straightforward; try larger office blocks first – a friendly commissionaire might allow you access to the roof.

641 Distant view
Some of the grander monuments and buildings can be seen from miles away. At Chartres in France or Salisbury in England it is for instance worth a drive into the surrounding country in order to shoot across the fields. Try for an interesting foreground frame, or use a telephoto as in **590**.

642 Skywards
When the dominant impression of a building is soaring verticals, use the camera in the vertical (portrait) format.

643
To create an impression of the way Gothic cathedrals seem to aspire to the heavens, accentuate their soaring height by moving in close with a wide-angle lens tilted upwards to emphasize converging verticals (see **300**). This approach is especially effective if the sun is poised above the spire – stop right down to turn the sun into a burst of light.

644 Grandeur
Formal, classical buildings or monuments need a formal approach. For the strongest image, shoot from directly in front rather than at an angle.

645 Islamic
Choose the slightly blue light of early morning to bring out the cool elegance of Islamic monuments; the effect will be enhanced if water is included in the shot. You can create a similar effect later in the day by using an 82A filter.

646 Colouring
If a monument or building is rather dull in colour, use the colour of sunlight early and late in the day to inject interest – or use coloured filters, with moderation.

647 Floodlight
Many monuments and buildings are lit by floodlight at night and it is worth returning after dark. All the surrounding clutter will be in shadow. If the floodlighting is fluorescent, see **360**.

648 Eliminating people
Many shots of great buildings and monuments are spoilt by crowds of people milling round. Avoid the crowds by getting up early. Alternatively, use a neutral density filter and a time exposure (camera on tripod) to make the crowds just disappear. Movement won't record if the exposure is in the region of 15–30 secs. An ND2 filter calls for an increase in exposure of the equivalent of $6\frac{2}{3}$ stops. So if normal exposure were $\frac{1}{4}$ sec at f16, with an ND it would be 26–27 seconds at the same aperture. Some precautions are however necessary. Exposures in excess of 1 sec can alter the colour response of film, and exposure needs to be computed by referring to the reciprocity failure table supplied with the film.

649
Don't allow any new interpretation of a monument or great building to mask its essential character. If the subject is totally unrecognizable in a photograph, the picture fails.

650
Don't include familiar objects such as clocks at the edge of the frame when shooting with a wide angle lens. The steep perspective will make them look horribly distorted.

651
Never tilt the camera up slightly to include the ceiling or the wall higher up. With the camera tilted, vertical lines in the picture will converge towards the top of the frame. You can sometimes use this effect deliberately to create an impression of great height. But you must tilt the camera significantly – any half-hearted tilt looks accidental. Verticals that converge downwards are not so disturbing, so you can tilt the camera when shooting down into an interior.

652 Small rooms
When photographing small rooms it can be difficult to get everything you wish into the picture. There are a number of ways of overcoming the problem: using a suitable wide-angle lens (between 20 and 28mm on a 35mm camera), if your camera accepts interchangeable lenses, being the most obvious and convenient. But see also **653–657.**

653
Another solution to the problem of photographing a small room (see **652**) is to back right into a corner. This not only gives you maximum shooting distance but often gives a more interesting shot as well, because you include two walls at an angle, not just one.

654
If photographing a small room, use a waist level or 90° viewfinder. Because you do not have to get behind the camera yourself, you can move the camera right into a corner or up against a wall.

655
Shoot the reflection of a small room in a mirror. This will give you a little extra in the picture – but photograph at an angle to the mirror which does not include you or the camera in the picture.

656
Stand on a stool or use a step ladder to gain extra height. If you need long exposures, use a firm table.

657
Photograph the room from outside, through a window or an open doorway.

658 Natural light
To retain the natural atmosphere of a room and minimize any technical problems, photograph by available light whenever possible even if it means long exposures, but beware of reciprocity failure – see end of tip 648.

659 Including the ceiling
Hold the camera perfectly level and use the vertical (portrait) format with a wide angle lens. Crop out unwanted areas at the printing stage. Avoid the temptation to tilt the camera upwards – see 300.

660 Shift lens
If you take interior photographs frequently, consider investing in a shift lens (see 301) or, better, a technical camera with a full range of movements. The latter is an expensive item, but it gives complete control over perspective.

661 Long exposure
For best-quality colour rendering when exposure is longer than 1 sec, use tungsten

film even when shooting in daylight, but remember to fit an 85 series filter over the lens. See also 662.

662
Tungsten film is much less prone to reciprocity failure (648) than daylight film. Remember you can empty interiors by means of long exposures – see also 648.

663 Metering
For accurate exposure, point the meter at the floor, unless the floor is heavily shaded or brightly lit, in which cases use incident or grey card readings – 147 and 160.

664 Dimmer switches
Make use of modern dimmer switches if fitted – they are useful for regulating exposure and general effects.

665 Wide open spaces
To make a room seem bigger than it is, shoot with a wide-angle from below waist level from a corner of the room.

666
Avoid mixing light sources if you can help it. If a room needs artificial light for proper illumination, wait until dark before shooting, or pull the curtains, so that you don't mix daylight and artificial light. If you do have to mix daylight with domestic (tungsten) lamps, shoot on daylight film – although the lamps will come out a warm orange colour, this is more acceptable than the blueness of daylight shot on tungsten film

667
Avoid including windows in an interior shot whenever possible – the difference in brightness between outside and inside is far too great for any film to handle and it is impossible to expose both of them correctly. If you do include a window in the shot, expose for the interior. But bear in mind that if your meter indicates that this will be over ⅔ stop more exposure than needed for the exterior, results will usually be unacceptable on colour slide film.

668
Avoid shooting in fluorescent light whenever possible. See **360**.

669
Beware of shadows cast by artificial lights outside the picture area. Because they have no visible source, they can look extremely odd.

670
Avoid cluttered foregrounds – move furniture around if you have to. The open floor space in the front of the shot is essential to lead the eye into the picture.

671 Mixed lighting
Turn mixed lighting to your advantage when a window is in the shot by photographing at twilight on tungsten colour film with the room lights on. The interior will come out naturally but the colour response of tungsten film will turn the view through the window deep blue – ideal for a glamorous but warm effect.

672 Room with a view
When the view outside is an integral part of the shot, try shooting on an overcast day to minimize the contrast between indoors and outdoors. To further reduce contrast point the camera down to exclude the sky, overexpose (by half a stop or so) and underdevelop.

673 Eliminating 'pools'
When domestic lamps are the main light source in a picture, fill in with diffused flash – point the flashgun at a white surface, such as a sheet, to reflect its light into the room. This prevents the lamps appearing as prominent pools of light. Ignore the flash for exposure calculations, but remember that if tungsten light film is loaded, you will be dealing with mixed light sources. The solution is to fit an 85B conversion filter over the flash output if the unit accepts one.

674 Table lamps
Table and standard lamps are terrific for creating atmosphere, so turn them on, even when shooting by daylight. Although mixed light sources are normally to be avoided, a few small, shaded lamps have little effect on colour balance, yet make all the difference to the impact of the picture. With an 82A filter over the lens to tone down the orangeness of the lamps, the result should be completely natural.

675 Firelight
Even a roaring open fire hardly shows up in an interior lit by daylight, yet an empty grate makes a whole room look lifeless. If a window is not in the shot, you can pull the curtains after taking your picture and expose the film again for a longish time – using multiple exposures – see Assignment **8** – so that the fire comes out brightly in the completed shot.

676 Killing reflections
Mirrors in the picture can show awkward reflections – parts of the room you do not want to show, or perhaps you and your camera or equipment. If you spray a mirror with water from a domestic plant spray just before you take a shot this will diffuse and blur the reflections so that they are not intrusive.

677 Everyday objects
You don't need intrinsically beautiful or unusual objects for effective still lifes. Look around your own home and you will find many potentially interesting subjects.

678 Something in common
If you want your pictures to be more than a random collection of objects, select your props for some unifying theme or feature. The traditional still life of fruit and wine glasses, for instance, has elements linked by their suggestion of a feast. But there are many, many ways in which your props can relate to each other – or you may choose to point the contrast between ideas they symbolize rather than things they represent.

679 Unfinished business
One way to create an intriguing still life is to give a suggestion of unfinished activity – the implication that the camera is eavesdropping, sneaking a quick look when someone has left the scene for a moment. For instance, in a desk-top scene include a half-written letter and a pen, just put down. If

you want to photograph a cup, fill it with steaming coffee, still swirling from being stirred – perhaps with a cigarette lying smoking in an ashtray.

680 Attention to detail
Always try to think of a few small details that will round off an image and give it extra punch. A shot of a cocktail glass should obviously include all the trappings, such as straws and colourful paper decorations – but it is the half-sliced orange on the table or the sprig of mint that really makes the shot.

681 Jumble props
Scour local jumble sales for props to add atmosphere and colour. Earthenware jars, for instance, are invaluable for shots of wholesome foods.

682 Backgrounds
A selection of material useful for backgrounds is essential if you do much still life photography. Try to build up a varied stock of coloured paper, squares of fabric of all textures and colours, plastic sheeting, wallpapers and laminates such as Formica.

683 Black velvet
For a completely neutral background when you want to photograph objects such as antique pottery, a piece of black velvet is ideal. It gives a dark, featureless background, devoid of shadows, that will not compete with your subject. What's more it will not suffer from crumpling, so you can take a piece of black velvet when you go out into the field.

684
Beware of specks of dirt, fluff and grease marks. They might seem tiny at the time, but they will stick out like a sore thumb in the photograph. All still lifes must be immaculately clean. You can get fluff off black velvet with sticky tape, fingermarks off glass and metal with acetone or surgical spirit, and an antistatic cleaning cloth (the type sold for LPs and spectacles) should clear most of the dust that clings to perspex

685
Watch out for
unpleasant
reflections when
photographing shiny
objects. In
particular, make
sure that the
reflection of the
camera does not
appear in the shot.
You can avoid such
problems by
pointing the camera
through a hole in
matt black card and
spraying the area of
the subject that
relfects the image of
the lens with a
cosmetic dulling
spray. This and
other sprays,
including instant
cobwebs, are
available from photo
dealers.

686 Coloured lights
For lively coloured back-
grounds, try using coloured
lights on white card, rather
than a coloured backing. Coloured gels for lights can be expensive, but this method of colouring the backing is far more
versatile – you can mix colours, put them where you want
and project colour on to any
background. Coloured card
cannot give the same sparkling effect. Use only heat-
resistant gels.

687 Scoop
The scoop is one of the most
useful of all still life settings,
particularly for single objects.
The subject rests on a large
piece of white Plexiglas (flexible plastic glass) or Formica,
which is curved up out of sight
behind it. This gives absolutely
no detail in the background yet
has the appearance of great
depth. The illusion of depth
can be enhanced by lighting
the front of the scoop with diffused light so that the background gradually disappears
into shadow.

688 Glass table
If you want to introduce all
kinds of special effects into
your backgrounds, invest in a
plate glass table. You can rest
your subject on the table and
shoot from above. Any type of
background you choose can
be put under the table and
your subject can float anywhere you like in the frame.
Just as advantageous, you can
light the subject from almost
any angle.

689 Light tent
For completely shadowless,
general diffused lighting,
ideal for all kinds of record
photographs and many natural
history subjects, construct a
light tent. Rig it up on a simple
wooden frame, using either
tracing paper or a plain white
sheet as the diffusing material.
Begin by using it outdoors, and
later experiment with artificial
lighting from various directions. If the material is a cotton
sheet, shoot with a pale blue
filter over the lens.

690 Natural settings
Backgrounds do not always
need to be created. Some of
the most effective still lifes use
a natural setting appropriate to
the subject, for example a
scrubbed wooden table as the
foil for simple farmhouse food.

691 Preparing food
Always make sure that food is in perfect condition – choose fruit and vegetables carefully, make sure the loaf or piecrust is baked just right. Seafood tends to lose colour when dry, so wet it thoroughly just before taking the photograph. With salad and fresh fruit, spray everything with a domestic plant spray to achieve a sparkling; fresh effect.

692 Glowing glass
To give a glass of beer or a bottle of whisky a golden glow, light it from underneath. In a piece of opaque card cut a hole the size of the base of the bottle, place the card on a glass table, put the bottle over the hole and place a light under the table. A white card placed behind a glass of liquid brightens the contents: this is the secret of lager ads.

693 Camera and lens
Reflex viewing is a boon for still lifes because of the need for accurate composing – see **5**. Specialists use a medium format SLR for maximum image quality, or a technical camera. Medium telephotos are best for most still lifes – you can fill the frame from some distance, leaving room for lights and other paraphernalia.

694 Improvising
Special light sources, such as flash 'fish fryers' and small spotlights are easy to improvise. See **990** and **1000**.

695 Hard edge
Two pieces of matt black card, placed out of frame on either side of a light-coloured subject, will prevent its edges being lost against a pale background in diffused light.

696 Highlights
Shiny objects need diffuse light, but a flashgun aimed through a small slit in black card (or a carefully aimed pen torch) can add a discreet highlight. To eliminate unwanted highlights, see **685**.

697 Fun reflections
Cut-out silhouettes stuck over a light source produce myriad images on the highlights of multiple reflective objects such as water droplets.

698
Don't spray water anywhere near electrical leads or flashguns.

699
Don't forget that with strongly directional lighting, shadows may be much darker in the picture than they appear to the naked eye. Examine the shadows in the viewfinder and if they appear dark, use hand mirrors, shiny metal or even white paper to reflect light into the shadow areas.

700
Never use auto extension tubes in combination: it can damage the camera linkages.

701
Don't be fooled by the term 'micro' on lenses. They are simply macros.

702
Don't bother with the split image focusing aid when viewing close-up: it will not function. Use the matt portion of the screen instead.

703 Remember
Camera movement is greatly magnified in close-up.

704
For impact, close-ups should be pin-sharp, so use a slow, fine grain film.

705
If using non-automatic extension tubes, you have to stop down manually before exposure. Auto tubes eliminate this problem, but see **700**.

706
Extension tubes can be used with lenses of different focal length for different effects.

707 Focusing
The simplest way to focus with extension tubes, supplementary close-up lenses and even macro lenses is to move the camera back and forth. With reversing rings this is the only way. Bellows are easiest to focus; see **904–905**.

708 Supplementaries
The most useful supplementary close-up lenses are + 3 and + 2 dioptres. Anything weaker has too little effect, anything stronger is excessive.

709
If you combine supplementaries, use the more powerful lens nearest the camera.

710
Supplementaries have different effects with different lenses – so experiment.

711
Quality falls off with the more powerful supplementaries: use the weakest one possible.

712 Spacing bracket
This device not only helps you keep the subject the right distance from the lens, but determines the picture area.

713 Four-legged stand
This holds the camera pointing vertically downwards, useful not only for copying objects that have to be flat, such as documents, but other subjects where square angles are important. The cheaper alternative is a clear plastic cone.

714 Spirit level
Check horizontal alignment by means of a spirit level.

715 Close-up stand
Not only camera but subject needs to be held still in much close-up work. It may be worth constructing a wooden stand on which camera and subject can both be attached.

716 Exposure
TTL metering solves most of the exposure problems caused by

fitting close-up attachments. The further the lens from the film, the more exposure is required to compensate for light fall-off. If your camera does not have TTL metering, increase exposure by the square of the lens-to-film plane distance divided by the square of the focal length.

717 Extra illumination
In the field, a sheet of silver foil or space blanket can be useful for throwing extra light on to the subject. See also **277**.

718
Ring flash provides shadowless, general illumination highly suitable for record-type shots and particularly of flowers in the field where movement has to be frozen. See also **553**.

719
Experiment with pocket mirrors, shiny spoons or a pen torch to provide extra local illumination for tiny subjects.

720
An Anglepoise or other adjustable desk lamp fitted with a floodlamp will provide useful illumination for most small close-up subjects. Remember to use tungsten film, or a conversion filter – see **357**.

721 Light quality
Strong shadows look bad in close-up. Generally use bright, diffuse lighting; if not possible, use fill-in. See **247** and **719**.

722
For a truly sparkling image, try backlighting the subject against a dark background.

723 Backgrounds
If using a pale background, make sure it carries no distracting shadows. Eliminate them by using a light tent – **689** – or by raising the subject above the background on a glass sheet and lighting from above with a pair of lights angled at 45°. See also **552**.

724
To tonally separate a subject from its background, light the background strongly.

725
Sky backgrounds can be darkened with a polarizer – see **371**.

726 Preview
To gain an impression of what a close-up will look like without setting up the camera, view the subject through a household magnifying glass.

727 Liquids
Liquids can be fascinating close-up subjects. Experiment with droplets on different surfaces. A smear of petroleum jelly will make most liquids accumulate into droplets. Add colour by dying the liquid, or with a colourful background.

728
Don't attempt high-magnification shots of subjects which have depth: in the macro range, depth of field really is negligible.

729
Don't just think of small objects as close-up subjects. Try moving in close on large subjects.

730
Avoid backgrounds which are lighter than close-up subjects. A much darker background is usually most successful.

731
Consider whether your subject will be recognizable in a close-up shot. Often, the close-up effect changes radically. If so, try a different camera angle.

732
Don't use a telephoto lens on a hazy day unless you want to increase the haze effect. A skylight filter may help counter haze.

733
Don't let salty spray dry on the camera. If possible, wipe it off straightaway with a cloth dampened in fresh water. Lenses should always be protected by a skylight or UV filter (see **354, 355**) when photographing at sea. Never rub a salty lens – you could scratch it.

734
Don't risk getting a camera drenched. A 'weatherproof' camera will withstand a shower, but probably not submersion.

735 Mist and haze
Take advantage of the way in which haze gives different tonal values to objects silhouetted at varying distances from the camera.

736
Use filters to emphasize haze (see **386**) or to cut through it (see **354, 355** and **383**). Haze usually builds up through the day; to minimize it, shoot early.

737 Fog
In thick haze and fog, contrast is of course drastically reduced. Introduce it by including some strong foreground element. Back- or side-lighting often overcomes the problem.

738
Fog mutes colours. Make use of this to set off a brightly coloured foreground object against the background.

739 Exposure
Bracket(**161**)by half to one stop either side of metered exposure in fog and mist: totally accurate exposure is impossible in these conditions. Slight overexposure will make mist look whiter.

740 Camera protection
Protect your camera from rain, spray, dust or snow by putting it in a plastic bag. Cut an opening for the lens and fasten the plastic firmly all round the lens barrel with an elastic band. Then either seal the open end, operating the camera through the bag, or keep one hand inside and one outside.

A lens hood must be used in conjunction with this assembly to help shield the lens itself. A skylight filter (**354**) is the standard item for lens protection, normally kept in place all the time. In adverse conditions, it is vital. If the filter gets splashed or dirty just before you need to take a shot, simply take it off. It is difficult to clean a filter quickly without smearing.

741 Snow
Two stops extra exposure is required. See **154**.

742
Falling snowflakes in the near to middle distance will record as streaks at speeds of 1/60 or slower with a standard lens.

743
Bring out the texture of snow by shooting against the light. Frontal lighting makes snow look dead. However, this effect can be used to emphasize the bleakness of a snowy landscape.

744 Sub-zero
In frosty weather, be alert for detail shots: icicles, frost patterns on windows and so on.

745
In heavy frost – say below 14°F (– 10°C) – skin can freeze to the metal parts of a camera. Tape such surfaces over, and see **747**.

746 Winterizing
If you and your camera are to encounter temperatures below freezing point, run a simple test to see how the mechanics will respond. Set a freezer to the anticipated temperature, and leave the camera in it overnight. If the controls are sluggish, consider having the camera winterized – an expensive, specialist operation which entails removing the standard lubricants. Have them restored before normal use. See also **747**.

747 Arctic
Beware of film becoming brittle – the effect of low temperatures and low humidity combined – in true arctic conditions, i.e. temperatures in the region of – 20°F (– 30°C) or lower. Keep the camera warm under your anorak. See **753**.

748 Batteries
Temperatures around and below freezing point may surprise you with their ability to sap batteries of power. An obvious sign of this is sluggish functioning of the information display in the viewfinder. At worst, all an automatic's functions will cease. Carry spare batteries, or a selenium cell meter (**850**). See also **746**.

749 Film speed
Extreme heat and cold will not, as some people expect, alter the effective speed of film.

750 Above 120°F (49°C)
In these conditions keep cameras and equipment in insulated bags, or wrap them in foil – otherwise metal parts could burn the user. If possible, keep equipment in shade, or off the ground, where it is hotter than a foot or two higher. Above 120°F, amateur film should be stored at controlled temperatures (see **68**) otherwise there is a risk of colour balance being affected. Carry the film in a Thermos or insulated bag until needed.

751 High humidity
In tropical and other extremely damp climates, pack cameras and equipment in sealed containers with silica-gel bags to absorb harmful moisture.

752 Steamy atmosphere
Keep the camera warm. Steam from a natural geyser, or even a kitchen kettle, can mist your lens. Sometimes you can demist a lens by holding it in a draught.

753
Don't jerk film when winding on in extreme cold (see **747**). Arctic temperatures make film brittle and likely to snap. Wind on smoothly and very slowly. Avoid using a motor drive.

754
Don't take a camera into a warm building or vehicle from cold outside temperatures. Moisture will condense on the lens. Leave the camera outside, or if you have to take it in allow time for it to warm up before use.

755
Take care not to breathe on the viewfinder in cold weather. Hold your breath as you raise the camera to your face, otherwise you could mist the viewfinder, or in low temperatures leave a frozen film of condensation.

756
Never use grease to seal opening parts of a camera against sand or dust. It can work its way into the interior, causing considerable mischief. Likewise, don't put grease on flash terminals: it may deaden connections.

757
Beware of the effect of the Earth's rotation in long exposures at night. The moon and stars record as streaks at time exposures longer than 10 secs.

758
Avoid flat-looking night picures by trying to include reflections of lights in water – or any reflective surface. This is almost the only way to achieve depth in night shots.

759
Watch for coloured smoke when taking fireworks pictures. It can record as an unattractive, blotchy colour cast due to drifting while the shutter is open. If you see smoke, put on the lens cap until it passes.

760 Dust and sand
Beach sand is the most common cause of camera breakdown. Exposure to heavy clouds of dust encountered when dirt track driving is potentially as harmful. Basic precautions are vital in such conditions – see **354**. If you encounter a true dust- or sandstorm, seal the opening parts of the camera, plus the flash sockets, with tape, and see **740**.

761 Night photography
Use the fastest lens and fastest film available to you. Avoid, where possible, long exposures: these can cause fogging of bright lights, and reciprocity failure – see end of tip **648**.

762 Metering
A built-in meter, or a quality hand-held meter, will probably give readings of nighttime street scenes, floodlit sports events etc, but bracketing is still advisable (**161**). If the meter is clearly just failing to register, also bracket.

763
If there is no meter response at all, try readjusting the film speed setting. If for example you have loaded a 400 ISO film, turn the setting to 800, then 1600, then 3200 (and higher if such a setting is available). When the meter comes into action, work out the number of increments, and increase exposure accordingly. See **133**.

764
Highly sensitive meters are of course an asset in night photography, but remember they may well be misled by small, bright points of light, especially if against a dark background. Compensate by bracketing (**161**).

765 Film type
Night scenes that include artificial light sources generally record acceptably on daylight film, even if the colours do look warm. If true colour is vital, use tungsten film – but see **360**. Tungsten film makes light appear extra blue at dusk; and see **662**. Daylight film makes houselights look warm.

766 Artificial night
Shooting at dusk, just before total dark, makes pictures seem more 'nocturnal' than true after-dark exposure. See also **617**.

767 Trails
Put the camera on a tripod, set the shutter at B and record trails of light made by cars.

768 Lightning/fireworks
Point camera at the area of sky where the flash is likely to occur. Open the shutter. If subject is visible for 4–5 secs or longer, it will record even at medium aperture on medium-speed film. Multiple exposures are possible – just leave the shutter open, or put on the lens cap between exposures. Remember the background gets paler with every exposure.

769
Rockets make more successful fireworks pictures than static displays, which fog out. The longer the exposure, the more colours will bleach out.

ASSIGNMENTS

Projects for the camera

CARDBOARD COWBOY

You don't have to go out West to shoot a silhouette cowboy riding out of the sunset. With a little ingenuity, a roll of slide film, plus slide-copying equipment, you can create this, and a whole range of similar effects at home.

The secret is, of course, that the cowboy is not real. Cliff Feulner, who has developed this technique extensively, shot a slide of a cardboard cut-out and combined it with a slide of a rich, sunset sky. In the same way, he makes convincing silhouettes of anything from elephants to cathedrals.

To get the basic shape for a cut-out silhouette, look through books and magazines. When you find a suitable picture – as large, and with as simple an outline as possible – trace it out carefully. Then hold the tracing over a piece of thin, high-quality black card, obtainable from artists' suppliers, and go over the outline firmly with a ballpoint pen. Cut out the shape scored on the card using a sharp scalpel or craft knife.

The silhouette must be held in front of a bright, even light source – a light box for example or a glass table lit from beneath by reflected light. Both camera and silhouette need to be held firmly – the camera should be on a tripod and the silhouette stuck in place with clear sticky tape. And a close-up lens, such as a 105mm macro, makes life easier. The important point to remember is that the silhouette must be solid black, so expose for the light source, but give one stop extra exposure to ensure that the light source is burnt out.

When your silhouette is processed and mounted, you can combine it with a slide of a sunset sky, either taken especially, or from a stock of pictures already built up. The only requirement is that it should be colourful and striking – remember, the rest of the picture is black.

To combine the silhouette and sunset slides, sandwich them together, with the matt emulsion sides facing, holding them together with clear sticky tape. Photograph the sandwich either in a slide copier or projected from an enlarger, using normal copying techniques (tips **1282–1290**). The process of copying should increase contrast enough to ensure the cut-out is properly silhouetted.

To make effective silhouettes remember:
● A large shape is easier to cut than a small one, and any errors will be reduced in combinaton.

● The silhouette image should not be a close-up image, or the 'impossible' depth of field (**172**) will make the combination unconvincing.

● The viewpoint for the silhouette shot should be realistic, unless you want a surreal effect.

● **See also tips:** 607, 687, 694, 700, 723.

Equipment
● SLR
● Macro lens
● Tracing paper
● Scalpel (craft knife)
● Ballpoint pen
● Thin black art card
● Clear sticky tape
● Slide-copying equipment

The best way of photographing the silhouette is to place it on a glass table or a sheet of window glass. To light the silhouette, point a flashgun or an Anglepoise lamp at a piece of white card held at 45° beneath the glass, aiming for even, white illumination behind the cut-out you have chosen.

Match your silhouette and the sky carefully to make an effective picture. Here the cowboy's relaxed pose in the saddle goes well with the setting sun. Silhouettes can be especially effective if seen to either hide, tell or suggest a story that is relevant to the picture's setting.

ROMANTIC PORTRAIT

A soft, romantic approach to pictures of young girls can be most appealing, and few photographers are more adept at creating a romantic atmosphere than David Hamilton. This simple, but tender head and shoulders shot is typical of his work.

More than anything, this is a 'mood' picture. Hamilton's skill lies not so much in capturing the girl's personality, indeed any hint of personality might intrude on what is, essentially, an idealized picture of a young girl; the art is creating the air of dreamy sensuality.

The key to this mood is the soft lighting – in an indoor location, natural light from a window provides just that. It is no coincidence that Hamilton chooses to live in the South of France, where he is assured of excellent natural light for much of the year. Direct sunlight is too harsh and must be diffused.

Sunlight may be diffused by reflection from the sky, so north-facing windows are useful for this type of shot. But light reflected from the sky has a blue cast that can cause problems with colour balance. So a window that catches light reflected from a light-coloured surface, such as a whitewashed wall, is much better, and it is this type of light that David Hamilton uses. An alternative is to put a piece of tracing paper, or a white cotton sheet, over the window to diffuse the light. A similar effect can be created with bounced flash, but natural daylight is much cheaper, and easier to use.

Although the soft, low-contrast lighting is the key element of the mood, the simplicity of the background and the predominance of pastel colours are also significant. Romantic pictures need a dreamy feeling and any sharp detail or strong colour would intrude. The background should ideally complement the girl's skin colouring. Here a warm brown sheet of background paper is used, but a plain, painted wall would do equally well.

Finally, there is the girl herself. Again, like the background, the dress should be soft, simple and pale for the romantic portrait – or better still, the shoulders should be completely bare, as in Hamilton's picture. A natural, unmade-up look further enhances the softness; and the hair should likewise be simply arranged. With the subject glancing gently towards the camera, the effect is as complete as possible.

If you try to take romantic portraits:
● Have the shoulders and eyes slightly turned, and never flat on the camera.
● Use the hands to balance the chin in a profile shot.
● **See also tips:** 430, 448–478.

Equipment
● 35mm SLR
● 105mm lens
● Tracing paper
● Background paper

Soft lighting and muted, natural colours give this David Hamilton portrait a warm romantic glow. But a few unusually classical touches – the long bare neck, the plaits of hair tied like a wreath, and the woman's direct gaze – create an effect unsually striking for this type of shot.

Although the simplest way to get the soft light you need for romantic portraits is to use reflected sunlight, you can diffuse direct sunlight by covering a window with a large sheet of tracing paper. A sheet of background paper in a suitable pastel shade will disguise a distracting background.

KALEIDOSCOPE

Combining photographs is a well-tried technique, but here photo-artist Monique Fay has created an unusual and striking image by assembling four copies of the same photograph. Assembling the photographs is actually a straightforward process, indeed, Monique Fay was happy to leave it in the hands of a professional laboratory. The lab simply made four large transparencies from the original photo, two the right way round and two reversed, and then carefully cemented the edges together. The real effort went into planning the image and taking the original photograph.

You cannot simply use any photo to produce an image like this – the result would be a mess. Neither can you rely on cropping the picture to achieve the desired effect. The photo has to be right at the moment of taking. Yet the original scene that Monique Fay saw through the viewfinder was only a quarter of the final image. So she had to have a very clear idea of what the composite would look like before she took the picture.

The angle and placing of the dominant lines (the band of earth, the shades of grass) within the frame were crucial – they had to meet the edges of the frame at precisely the right places to give the right pattern. For such accurate framing, a reflex camera is essential, and Monique Fay used a Nikon F3, held at an angle of about 40° to the ground.

Getting a professional laboratory to cement four large transparencies together is extremely expensive – Monique Fay had it done this way because she wanted to reproduce the image many times. But you can make a composite like this much more cheaply if you only want one copy. Simply make, or have made, four matching prints from the original photograph – two with the film the right way up, two with it reversed – trim them, and mount them on card or board.

If you decide to make your own composites, watch these points:

● For the basic shot, look for strong lines and simple subjects.

● Keep the composition as simple as possible at the corners of the frame that are to meet – remember, every detail is multiplied four times.

● Try to arrange your design to 'frame' the centre of the diamond, leading the eye into the picture.

● Sketch the finished design before you shoot: this helps you work out the exact framing.

● Shoot on a tripod if possible. This way you can repeat the exact shot four times. With four slides, you can try out the design before printing.

● Try other patterns using four or more copies.

● **See also tips:** 5, 121, 1228–1277, 1282–1290.

Equipment
● Reflex camera
● Tripod
● Sketchbook and pencil
For one-off prints
● Scalpel or craft knife
● Metal ruler
● Stiff card or board
● Rubber-based gum

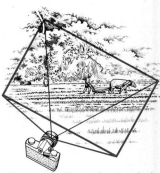

To create a diamond pattern in the composite, the camera must be held at an angle and this can make framing difficult – yet precise framing is essential. So draw out the final design on paper before you shoot and look carefully where the lines in the scene cross the edge of the frame.

By repeating the same image four times, Monique Fay has created a striking diamond pattern.

GARDEN CREATURES

Stunning wildlife shots like these are generally beyond the scope of the amateur. Stephen Dalton's shot of the tit frozen in flight and Heather Angel's picture of the dormouse are both products of years of experience. But if you have a suitable garden, there is no reason why you should not take good wildlife shots with no more than a basic SLR outfit.

The background is crucial – for the dormouse, Heather Angel has arranged a setting that is colourful and attractive yet completely natural, while the plain background to Stephen Dalton's shot shows off the action beautifully. So your first task is to find a suitable background in an area the creature frequents.

Then you must arrange to fire the camera without disturbing the creature. With bird shots, you may be able to use the house as a hide and shoot from behind the curtains, but in most situations it is better to operate the camera by remote control while you remain concealed in a convenient hide, such as the garden shed. For this you will need a motor drive and a remote control device – an air release is ideal.

The next task, and by far the most exacting, is to use bait to draw the creature into the frame. Baiting should not be undertaken lightly – it is the creature's food supply with which you are tampering. Take expert advice, but make sure the bait looks natural if it is to appear in the frame. And be patient; it may be days before the bait is taken regularly.

- For birds, hang up a hollow log stuffed with shelled nuts.
- For small mammals, leave a saucer of milk regularly.
- Flash helps to freeze and highlight the creature.
- **See also tips:** 255, 264, 313, 314, 319, 554–568.

Equipment
- 35mm SLR
- Telephoto (200 or 300mm)
- Tripod
- Air release
- Quality flashgun (or two)
- Patience

Heather Angel's dormouse shot was taken on a studio set, but you can shoot small creatures in the garden by firing the camera from a hide. Use bait to draw the creature into the picture area. Then, when it takes the bait regularly, set the camera on the tripod, focus, and retire to your hide to await the shot. This may take days. Use a pair of flashguns either side of the camera if the light is poor.

For his shot of the Great Tit, Stephen Dalton used a special high-speed flash to freeze it in flight, but provided the light is good, you can get acceptable shots without any special equipment. Hang the bait on a branch near the window, conceal yourself in the house and shoot as birds 'brake' to land.

MATCH POINTS

For amateurs, the exciting feature of major tennis tournaments is that it is usually possible to get almost as close to the game as the men of the press – close enough to get pictures like sports photographer Eamonn McCabe's superb shot of McEnroe.

But you need to get to the match early to be sure of a viewpoint near the centre of the court – just behind the press box – where you can shoot players at either end. From this position you can fill the frame for a full-length action shot with a medium telephoto, say 200mm. A lens any longer is unsuitable for action shots simply because the player moves out of the frame too quickly. Eamonn only uses a long lens – a 400mm, for instance – for close-ups of the players as they pause between games or wait for a service. A monopod provides the ideal support, taking up little room and allowing you to swivel the camera.

For the action shots of McEnroe and Jo Durie, a vertical format was essential to fill the frame. So Eamonn McCabe hand-held the camera, resting his arms on the barrier for extra steadiness. A high shutter speed both froze the action and reduced the effect of any slight movement of the lens.

With the McEnroe shot, the idea was to catch the peak of the action. To get this kind of shot, you need to ignore the game and simply follow the player in the viewfinder. It takes years of practice to fire the shutter at just the right moment – most people fire too late. But the best moment is just as the player draws his arm back – by the time the shutter fires, the ball should be shooting off the racket.

- Use a wide aperture to blur distracting backgrounds.
- Avoid motor drives – they may distract some players.
- **See also tips:** 116–119, 526–545.

Equipment
- SLR
- 200mm lens
- 64 ISO film for sunny day
- 200 or 400 ISO for dull day

For close-ups
- 400mm lens
- 1.5× converter
- Monopod

For close-ups of the players pausing between shots, a 400mm lens and a 1.5× converter make an ideal combination. Hand-held shots are impossible with this combination, and the best support is a monopod, a one-legged tripod that gives reasonable stability and some freedom of movement. For action-stopping shots like that of McEnroe (right), a 200mm lens, hand-held, is better. To catch the peak of the action, fire just as the racket arm comes back. But remember, expressions betraying great effort can make equally effective shots, as for example in Jo Durie's knife-edge backhand return, left.

WILD FLOWERS

On film, flowers all too often seem to lose their fragile charm – in fact many pictures of flowers are simply dull. The secret, as these two photographs show, is to get down to the level of the flowers and fill the frame.

The larger picture, taken by Bill and Claire Leimbach, shows this approach. The camera was moved right in to concentrate on a single orchid head. James Barrow, on the other hand, has included the whole plant in the smaller picture (below right); the shot is less immediately arresting, but no less attractive, capturing more of the flower's natural delicacy. The feeling of naturalness was enhanced by the inclusion of some of the woodland habitat.

To fill the frame with a single bloom, close-up equipment is necessary, but it did not have to be elaborate. James Barrow used a 55mm macro lens on a 35mm SLR, allowing him to focus less than a foot (0.3m) away. Extension tubes could have been used for exactly the same effect.

A plain background, with no distracting detail, is essential to most close-ups, so he chose a viewpoint slightly above the flower so that the grass beyond became the backdrop. There was no problem keeping it out of focus because the depth of field is so slight at this range. In fact, he had to stop the lens down to f11 to ensure the whole subject was in focus. A tripod and cable release kept the camera steady for the 1/15 sec exposure needed.

For the close-up of the single orchid head, the Leimbachs needed a more elaborate arrangement. A 35mm SLR was ftted with extension tubes and a standard lens so that it could focus on the flower just 3in (8cm) away. But extension tubes cut down the amount of light reaching the film considerably, and to achieve an aperture of f22 (necessary for adequate depth of field) the shutter speed had to be ¼ sec, even though the sun was bright.

With the camera this close to the subject, movement of the flower can be a real problem; the slightest tremor caused by movement in the wind comes out on film as unacceptable blur. Holding the camera steady on a tripod is, by contrast, no problem at all. The solution was to build a windbreak, taking care not to let its shadow fall on the orchid head.

When working at close range:
● Focus with care; depth of field is minimal.
● Use the narrowest aperture possible. ·
● Use the depth of field preview button (fitted to most SLRS) to check that everything necessary is in focus.
● When possible, keep the background in shadow.
● If you happen not to be able to erect a windshield, plant stiff wire in the ground and attach it to the flower stem.
● **See also tips:** 546–553, 700–731.

Equipment
● SLR with macro lens or extension tubes
● Tripod and cable release
● Home-made windbreak
● White card reflector

A macro lens or extension ring(s) (above left and right) allows focusing close enough to fill the frame as with the orchid (right).

The slightest movement caused by wind is the bane of close-up work in the field: what the human eye dismisses as too slight to notice, the lens will record as blur this close. The solution is a windbreak, a wire stiffener, or both used in conjunction.

FIGURES OF FUN

With Paddy Eckersley's picture the idea was to create a tongue-in-cheek version of Pandora's Box. To give an impression of energy bursting from the box, he shone a light through the bottom of the box and caught droplets of water from a plant spray by means of flash. The girl's pigtails held up by cotton complete the effect.

Pictures of people never need be unoriginal. The only special equipment required is imagination, a knack for improvisation, and perhaps a sense of fun. These are the qualities which produced Brian Griffin's stylish boatrail silhouette and Paddy Eckersley's 'Pandora's Box'.

The techniques for both shots were invented by the photographers specifically to create the required images; no textbook can tell you the secrets of original effects. In modern professional photography, success is based increasingly on the ability to experiment.

Brian Griffin wanted an ultra-clean, modern moonlight-on-water effect for his shot, so he crumpled aluminium foil on the floor behind the rail. Lights at either side threw the reflections on the backdrop.

Paddy Eckersley cut a hole in the 'table' and the bottom of the box and shone a light through from underneath to make it look as if the contents of the box were glowing. Cotton held up the girl's pigtails invisibly and droplets of water from a plant spray were caught in the flashlight to complete the scene.

Set-ups like these are difficult to achieve out of doors, so adapt a corner of a room to act as a studio and invest in a roll of background paper. Clean backgrounds are essential, and even the smoothest painted wall cannot match genuine photographic backing paper, the backdrop in both pictures.

- Don't allow the effect to overwhelm the subject.
- Keep items for pinning and fixing to hand: tape etc.
- Take advantage of reflective surfaces.
- **See also tips:** 681, 682, 686–688, 692, 970–1001.

Equipment
- Camera, preferably rollfilm, for easy composition
- A Polaroid back is particularly useful; you can see if your effects are working
- Lights – as many as you can collect. Be prepared to improvise, using domestic lamps, flash or photofloods
- Background paper
- Useful items for creating effects such as tape, pins, cotton, scalpel (craft knife)

It is important not to be carried
away by the excitement of special
effects. Brian Griffin's picture
works not simply because of the
spectacular lighting effect but
because of the meticulous care
that has gone into arranging the
figures in the foreground.

DOUBLE TAKE

Few would doubt, looking at this characteristic Chris Alan Wilton shot of a goldfish and the moon, that there was some trick photography involved. But the trick is much simpler than most would suspect.

Chris Alan Wilton achieved the effect by making two exposures on the same frame, one of the fish and one of the moon. Double exposures used to be mistakes made by absent-minded photographers, but now they form the basis of the majority of special effects seen in advertisements and films. Once mastered, double exposure techniques can be used to create a range of bizarre, often beautiful effects.

The main problem with double exposures is ensuring the images fall in the right places on the frame, without overlapping. If each shot has a completely black background, as in the goldfish and moon shot, exact placing is much easier to achieve. So before trying anything elaborate, try combining subjects on black backgrounds.

Because of the need for perfect alignment, this shot cannot easily be taken on anything but a reflex or studio camera. If you use an SLR, you really need a focusing screen with a grid pattern marked on it, rather than the standard microprism screen. The grid helps you to locate each image in the frame.

A further problem with double exposures is that you never see the images combined until the film is processed. So it is always worth making an accurate sketch of the combination and the position of the two images beforehand.

A third problem is that many cameras will not allow you to expose the same frame twice, even deliberately. However, it is possible to 'fool' a camera into taking double exposures as follows: after taking the first exposure, turn the rewind knob on the top of the camera to ensure the film is under tension. Then press the sprocket release button as you would when rewinding, and gently advance the wind-on lever to cock the shutter. If you can, hold the rewind lever to ensure the film does not move.

To achieve a photo like Chris Alan Wilton's, the camera needs to be on a tripod for precise composition. For the first exposure, he draped a black cloth behind the fish tank and lit only the goldfish. The shot of the moon is actually another slide, and the second exposure was made by replacing the camera's lens with a duplicating set-up (see tips **1282–1290**).

If you want to try double exposures:
● Work meticulously to ensure that the images are pefectly aligned.
● Halve the normal exposure except when shooting against a black background.
● **See also tips:** 189–193, 683, 694, 788, 1282–1290.

Equipment
● SLR
● Tripod
● Grid square focusing screen
● Slide copier
● Paper and pencil
● Black velvet

The simplest way to make double exposure pictures is to shoot the two subjects against a black background. For the shot of the goldfish, Chris Alan Wilton draped a black velvet cloth behind the fish tank. The night sky provided the suitable background for the moon. The moon shot could have been taken 'live', but in fact it was easier to use a stock slide and copy set-up.

PAINTING WITH LIGHT

Lights need not be restricted to simply illuminating the subject – you can literally 'paint with light', as London photographers Lawrence Lawry and Paddy Eckersley show in these pictures, to produce spectacular night-time shots. There is a large element of surprise, because you cannot tell what the result will be until you process the film, but when it works, the results can be impressive.

For these pictures, the photographers used two light sources, flash and torchlight – three if you count the twilight glow in the picture below. In each picture, the torch creates swirling patterns that criss-cross the frame like glowing spaghetti, and the flash illuminates the people.

For the picture below right, Paddy Eckersley chose a sloping path on London's Primrose Hill, using the incline to get the torch zigzagging down the frame. He decided where to place the figure and set up his tripod while it was still light, and then took regular light readings until it was dark enough to leave the shutter open for one minute. Then with the lens set to f11 for adequate depth of field, he locked

Equipment

- Camera and tripod
- Electronic flash and pen torch
- Red filter

A dozen circles of pen torches shot through a red filter, then a brief flash exposure without the filter completed this shot.

the shutter open. The model was already sitting on the bench as he fired off the flash from a portable unit to illuminate her. As soon as she saw the flash, she stood up and switched on the torch. The photographer followed her as she carried the torch to the next chosen spot, where he fired another flash. And so the two proceeded on up the hill.

Only when Paddy had achieved the effect he wanted did he hurry back down the hill to the camera and finally close the shutter.

If you try this technique yourself, expect to waste some film:

● Expose and process at least one test roll of film before you set up an elaborate shot.
● Try a few test runs in the garden to get the exposure balance right.
● If you fire the flash more than once, make sure that the unit is the same distance from the subject for each flash.
● Take advantage of the exposure latitude of colour negative film.
● **See also tips:** 255, 263, 264, 265, 284, 648.

Equipment
● Camera and tripod
● Portable flash
● Household torch

With a long time exposure at night, you can 'paint' intriguing patterns with torches and a portable flash unit.

HAND COLOURING

Hand colouring of black and white prints virtually disappeared after colour print film became widely available, but recently there has been a revival of interest in this old technique. Some are attracted to hand colouring for its old-fashioned look; others for the soft hues and control over colour rendering.

Helena Zakrzewska-Rucinska specializes in hand colouring, sometimes working on her own photographs, sometimes tinting old material from decades back. But the range of effects that can be achieved by hand colouring is enormous and the two pictures here show but two aspects of her work.

If you want to hand colour prints, it is best to avoid pictures with large dark areas, because the colour won't take in these areas – unless, as with the dog picture, it makes sense to leave the dark area uncoloured. It is also better to use prints made on fibre-based rather than resin-coated paper.

You can use a variety of colouring materials, but the simplest to use are water-based photographic dyes, applied with cotton wool swabs and fine paintbrushes. To allow the dye to spread evenly, soak the print in water first when you are tinting large areas. If you want to tint two or more large areas, colour one area, then go over it carefully with rubber-based masking lacquer (available from art suppliers) and resoak the print to colour the next area.

- After soaking, dry off excess water with blotting paper.
- If you make a mistake, you may be able to soak it out.
- Work quickly to finish before the print dries.
- Wear rubber gloves when using cotton wool swabs.
- **See also tips:** 1168–1199.

Materials
- Photographic retouching dyes
- Selection of paintbrushes
- Cotton wool swabs and buds
- Scalpel or craft knife
- Mixing palette
- Rubber-based masking lacquer

Hand colouring usually depends on subtlety for its effect, so don't mix the colours too strong – even in the dog picture, the tints are fairly muted. Work with dilute dyes and build up the colour layer by layer rather than trying to achieve the right effect in one. When mixing the dye, add it drop by drop to a small quantity of water. Don't be afraid to leave areas uncoloured. Notice how effective it was to leave the dog black. Choose prints with this type of consideration in mind.

1 Apply rubber-based masking lacquer to dyed areas.

2 Soak the print in water for at least five minutes.

3 Colour large areas with dye-soaked cotton wool swab.

4 Tint in details with a fine paintbrush.

SHOOTING STARS

Dramatic lighting, brilliant stage effects, charismatic performers – rock concerts seem to guarantee the photographer exciting shots. But as rock photographer Liz Hollingworth demonstrates, getting the best from the subject calls for a strong technique and not a little imagination.

The obvious problem the photographer encounters at rock venues is lack of light. The stage area might seem brilliantly lit, but for photography, light levels are barely adequate. Liz Hollingworth always loads her cameras with fairly fast film – usually 400 ISO Tri-X for black and white and 200 ISO Ektachrome for colour push-processed so that it can be shot at 400 ISO.

Although the light is generally poor, there is usually tremendous contrast, more than any film can cope with. But there is no need for the background to be well exposed. Indeed, it is often better if distracting details at the back of the stage are thrown into shadow. So expose for the performers and allow the background to go black.

Unfortunately, the light displays can change so rapidly that it is impossible to work from accurate meter readings from the skin tones all the time. Liz Hollingworth sets the shutter to 1/60, usually enough to stop camera shake, and then adjusts the aperture to suit the colour of the light display for each shot.

If you want to shoot the stars:
● Make sure you are allowed to use a camera.
● Fit a telephoto zoom to follow the performers as they move quickly around the stage.
● Get as close to the stage as possible.
● Rock concerts rely on extravagant lighting effects for their impact, so shoot in colour and take advantage of special effects filters such as starbursts.
● **See also tips:** 64–66, 313, 315, 376–378, 380.

● 35mm SLR
● Telephoto zoom (70–200mm) for shots of individual performers
● Wide-angle for whole stage shots
● Spot meter (ideally)
● Range of special effects filters

Shots of rock stars benefit from any little touch of glamour you can give them. So take advantage of special effects filters like starbursts, rainbows and multiprisms.

When shooting rock stars, try to vary your viewpoint as much as possible – shooting from directly in front of the stage it is easy to shoot full-face shots, but profiles can be equally effective as the shot of Toyah Willcox (top right) shows. Expose for the performer and let the background disappear in shadow as in the shot of Elton John (below right) and use a starburst to catch flashes of light (top, far right). A shot of the whole stage with a wide-angle sets the scene nicely (left) – though of course it lacks the impact of the close-ups.

BEACHCOMBER

If you enjoy collecting sea shells, why not photograph them then and there, on the sea shore? To do them justice, take the trouble to organize them into a collage, like Michael Freeman's colourful crab. It's a particularly free-and-easy form of still life to tackle because if you make the collage at least 2ft (0.6m) across, you should have no trouble filling the frame of the average 35mm SLR fitted with a standard lens focused at the closest focusing distance; no need for special close-up equipment.

Build up a large and varied collection of shells before even attempting a collage; however, it is worth planning the design roughly at an early stage, so you can collect shells with certain colours and shapes in mind. In general, small, colourful shells, rather than large, impressive shells, give the most scope. If you do pick up large shells, select the flattest types. They fit into patterns more easily than lumpy shells; notice that the only large shells used by Michael Freeman are scallops.

Before starting work on the collage, make a detailed drawing of the way you would like to see it turn out. Try to estimate how many shells you will need for each part of the pattern – you may find you have not enough of one shell type to fill the desired area, and this means changing the design. It is easier to do this on paper than with shells themselves.

Find a dry, flat area of sand, sheltered from wind. Better, work on a tray of sand, away from the beach altogether. Rule a grid pattern on the drawing, and transfer this to the sand by laying cotton or string across it; use the grid as reference for getting the basic proportions right.

Before laying down the shells, clean them in water, allow them to dry properly, and brush away stray grains of sand. Sort them into different colours and sizes and keep them in flat piles so you can tell at a glance how many of each you have. Take time building up the collage, working on one area at a time. Lay the shells with tweezers: fingers are surprisingly clumsy for this type of operation.

When the collage is ready, set the camera up on a tripod as near to vertically above the collage as possible. Frame up carefully and take an incident light reading (**147**) for most accurate exposure. If the lighting is strongly directional, use a white reflector to fill in shadows.

● Shoot out of doors, using natural light: a bright but overcast day gives best colour saturation.
● Bracket exposures (**161**) and try alternative framings.
● **See also tips:** 677–731.

Equipment
● Pencil, paper
● String
● Paintbrush and tweezers

Use tweezers to place the shells – fingers are too clumsy.

Before you photograph the collage, give it a careful brush over.

PHOTO-ESSAY

You're visiting a foreign city for the first and perhaps only time, yet there's just a day or two to get a set of pictures that sum up the place. It's a task that photo-journalists often face. One of the most effective solutions is to create a photo-essay like this Mike Freeman set on Hong Kong.

The idea of creating a photo-essay concentrates your approach and helps you to shoot effectively in the time available. But you need to work out in advance what you want to photograph – scan the guidebooks and make a list.

Try to think in terms of the combined effect rather than in single images. Not every shot has to be stunningly creative – some can be record shots included to show the context or make a point – referred to as 'point' shots by photo-journalists. The selection should be balanced so that no particular aspect receives undue weight – unless, of course, you want it to. The selection should be varied as well.

- Vary your viewpoint, using different scales and lenses.
- Use the vertical format as well as the horizontal.
- Vary the spot where you locate the centre of interest in the frame.
- Shoot at different times of day, in different light.
- Mix 'point' shots with creative shots.
- **See also tips: 390–400, 619–651, 689.**

Equipment

Lightweight camera outfit:
- SLR
- Lenses: 24 or 28mm, 50mm and 105mm plus converter
- Electronic flash
- Lightweight tripod
- Filters: 81A/B, polarizer
- Films of one brand

In his essay on Hong Kong, Mike Freeman has achieved, as much as possible in five shots, a balance between people, places and things. A shot of the city lights on Hong Kong island from Kowloon captures some of the allure and glamour of this teeming oriental city (below).

The colourful traditional theatre is an obvious but important subject (right). Don't neglect this type of shot even if it seems uncreative'; it is a vital part of the overall picture created by the essay.

Scenes away from the main tourist attractions are important too. The restaurant (below) may be unglamorous, but it is a typical feature of Hong Kong life. The shot of the people on the boat combines an image of everyday life with the bustle of the busy waterfront.

Look for an unusual but effective leading image like this shot of the lobster on a table on a floating restaurant: it sums up much of the romantic appeal of Hong Kong.

BIRTHDAY PARTY

Appealingly photogenic though they may be, children are notoriously difficult subjects with which to work. Anthea Sieveking (who specializes in child photography) finds children's parties can be a nightmare for the serious photographer who is caught unprepared.

If you are to work effectively at a children's party, you must be absolutely sure of your equipment so that you never waste time fiddling with exposure and focusing controls. While you are making adjustments, you could miss the perfect expression – or the mischievous five-year-old pouring ice cream in your camera bag. Even changing lenses can be a distraction, so work with a single lens – ideally a 105mm. Don't bother with a zoom; if you need to alter the framing, move.

Flash can destroy the atmosphere – and gives rather flat results anyway – so load the camera with fast film and shoot by available light wherever possible. Set the exposure controls, using an incident light reading (see tip **147**), before the party, and only alter them to achieve specific effects.

At first, children will be fascinated by the camera and will play up to it in the worst possible fashion. Show them how it works – even let them look through the viewfinder – and the novelty will soon wear off. Then you can begin to watch for shots.

To catch the best moments:
● Make three exposures for every shot – the expression will be different in each one, and it is the expression more than anything that makes the shot.
● Take your pictures while the children are involved in some activity, such as blowing candles out.
● Concentrate on individual children.
● **See also tips:** 227, 497, 498

Equipment
As basic as possible:
● SLR or 35mm compact
● 105mm lens
● Fast film

These two shots show just how worthwhile it can be making at least a couple of exposures for every situation. The first shot (above) is pleasant, but the perfect moment – when the whistle is fully extended – is only caught by the second shot (main picture, opposite).

Use fast film and shoot by available light wherever possible – flash would have destroyed the atmosphere of this hallowe'en party scene (left).

RESTORING AN OLD PHOTO

If you come across an old photo when clearing out a cupboard, don't throw it away, even if it is crumpled and torn. With relatively simple treatment, it can be restored to its former glory, as retoucher Roy Flooks has demonstrated with this turn-of-the-century piece.

The secret is to make a copy and work on that. Copying is simply a matter of taking a picture of the print, and the simplest way to do this is to fix the camera on a copy stand fitted with lamps.

If the print is curved and torn, like this one, lay it under a sheet of glass when shooting the copy. Unfortunately, glass does present problems with reflections, so keep the lights at as low an angle as possible and if there are still reflections, point the camera lens through a hole cut in a sheet of black card or board.

The print that Roy Flooks worked on had faded over the years, and a blue filter over the lens restored some of the lost contrast. The effect of yellow stains can be reduced with a yellow filter if they are on light areas, with a blue filter if they are on dark areas.

Any remaining blemishes have to be removed by hand retouching – that is, inking in and bleaching out blemishes. Ideally, this should be done on the copy negative, but if it is too small to work on, use a new print made from the copy negative.

When retouching:
● Bleach away large, dark stains by dabbing with cotton wool balls or buds soaked in Farmer's Reducer.
● Knife away small, dark spots with a scalpel (craft knife).
● Retouching dye on a fine brush covers white spots.
● **See also tips:** 160, 381–386, 1168–1199.

Equipment
For copying:
● Camera
● Purpose-built copy stand OR
● Improvised stand and lights
● Glass sheet
● Black card
● Filters
For retouching:
● Magnifying glass
● Retouching dyes
● Bleach (Farmer's Reducer)
● Cotton wool buds and balls
● Scalpel (craft knife)
● Fine paintbrush

To establish the exposure for the copy, take an incident light reading. Lighten dark stains with a filter of the same colour; darken light stains with a filter of a complementary colour.

The Tower Bridge Photographic C

Retouching properly requires considerable skill, but if you take meticulous care, you can probably disguise the worst blemishes. When mixing the dye, try it on an old piece of paper first to ensure it is the right shade to blend in perfectly with the area of the print being retouched.

GROUP PRACTICE

Group portraits used to be the dullest of all assignments for the photographer, conjuring up images of football teams and wedding parties in formal rows. But the demands of the popular music industry have shown just what can be done with the group shot. Both these pictures, by Brian Griffin (main shot) and Gered Mankowitz, show a group of four young men – but how different they are.

Brian Griffin's shot of the group on the beach was for an album cover. He is best known for his strikingly original portraits, but he is also in demand for album cover shots, and this shot, although less dramatic than some of his work, shows his characteristic skill in handling light.

In this type of shot the aim is not simply to record the faces of the members, nor to say much about their personalities. Rather, it is to create an identity or 'image' for them – often simply a device for drawing them together. In Brian's shot, the image, a combination of cool moodiness and artistic temperament, is established largely by the setting. Grey seas and grey skies are always heavy with 'atmosphere', but the sky needs a touch of light and shade for the picture to have the maximum impact.

The position of the figures is also crucial. Shots like these depend on a sense of isolation, difficult to achieve with four people. Brian Griffin's solution was to have them standing apart, silhouetted, staring out to sea, and leave a great expanse of sky above to create a sense of space. But to get silhouettes in this kind of light, even against such a bright background, called for careful exposure – and the beach had to be wet to catch the reflection of the sky.

In Gered Mankowitz's shot, the setting is irrelevant and the aim was to give one of the group a more prominent role. The mirror proves a simple and effective device, drawing the three members of the group and the leader together neatly.

If you want to experiment with group shots:
● Look for a device to draw them all together.
● Don't feel they have to look at the camera.
● Concentrate on the overall 'image'.
● **See also tips:** 436–443; and Assignment **7**.

Equipment
● Camera: preferably rollfilm to make composition easier and to ensure top quality
● Medium telephoto: to ensure you can frame all the group without unpleasant distortion of perspective – unless you deliberately choose this effect
● Tripod
● Useful props and costumes – similar (stylish or outrageous) clothes, or even hairstyles, can draw the group together well

Group shots need something to draw the members together visually – in Gered Mankowitz's shot, it is the mirror, held at an angle to give the shot a little excitement. If there is no particular image you want to create, look for simple devices like mirrors to unite the group.

Brian Griffin's shot was designed
to capture the essence of the
group's image, as well as to take
an attractive picture of the album
cover. The choice of setting is
crucial, yet often it is the details
that make or break a shot. The
seagulls, which seem so natural,
had to be attracted with fresh fish.

Wintry conditions can reward the photographer with fantastically beautiful effects; but to catch frost or snow at their best, rise early, before they melt.

Some frost effects are so spectacular, like the iced trees below, that provided you frame up thoughtfully, the shot is ready-made. A clean background is important, however, and a piercing blue winter sky can be ideal, particularly if the blue is strengthened with a polarizing filter. If any of the subject is in shadow, use an 81B filter to reduce blueness.

But the beauty of frost and snow is just as likely to be contained in relatively small details, noticed only by the observant. Look for frost patterns on leaves or tiny icicles on plants; isolate them from their backgrounds and shoot against the sun for glitter.

To give your photography direction and purpose, adopt the collector's mentality and enjoy a continuing assignment:

● Just as with frost and snow, build up a series of detail shots of any objects that fascinate you personally – from post boxes to manhole covers.
● Shoot a subject at different times of day.
● Return to photograph country scenes at different seasons.
● Catalogue portraits of children as they grow.

EQUIPMENT

Assessing one's needs ● Buying wisely

BUYING CAMERAS

770
Don't go on the advice of staff in your local camera dealer, however helpful they may be. Ask around to gauge the opinion of someone who has actually used the type of camera you want to buy. And always scan the photographic press for comparative test reports.

771
Be suspicious of ultra-low prices when buying mail-order – they may not include the battery, neck-strap and lens cap that come with a camera from a more expensive supplier.

772
Avoid buying a camera on a Saturday morning when the shop is overcrowded – you may not get the help you deserve.

773 Practical choice
No camera, no matter how expensive, will turn you into a good photographer overnight. So when you are deciding which camera to buy, get straight to the practical qualities you really need – forget about buying this or that camera because you have noticed that some famous photographer uses it. Make a list of the facilities you need for the pictures you want.

774 Hooks v looks
As a rule, styling is only an important consideration in snapshot cameras. In more complex cameras, practical qualities are paramount. If you take photography seriously, buy a camera for its specifications, and the way it feels in the hand, not for its looks.

775 Accessories
Before you make your final choice, make sure that the camera accepts all the accessories you are likely to use in future.

776 How much?
When trying to decide how much to spend on a new camera, work out the maximum you can afford, then halve it. Spend the difference on film – even the best camera is useless without film. Remember, the price of a quality SLR will only buy you 25 rolls of Kodachrome.

777 Useful features
Every extra feature tends to bump up the cost of a camera. Be sure that the money you are spending is giving you genuinely useful features such as a quality lens or increased exposure control, rather than gimmicks such as built-in motorized film winders.

778 Buying into a system
Buy the cheapest model from the range of one of the big 35mm SLR systems if you think your interest in photography may mushroom, but you are not yet sure, or you simply cannot afford a more versatile model. This way, the lenses and accessories you buy for your camera body, however modest, will not become unusable when you trade up to a more sophisticated model in the same system. For example, the cheapest camera in the Nikon range, the Nikon EM, takes all the same lenses as the professional's Nikon, the F3. See also **7, 4–6, 8–10.**

779 Budget SLRs
For the photographer who wants a reliable basic 35mm SLR (see **4–6**), but has no intention of buying any more photographic gear, budget SLRs such as those made by Fujica are excellent value.

780 Exposure systems
If you can afford a top 35mm SLR, choose one that gives the exposure system best suited to your needs – manual, shutter- or aperture-priority, or multi mode. See **781–784.**

781 Manual
A non-automatic exposure 35mm SLR gives you complete control, but is slow to use. So it is ideal for a slow, studied approach – and perhaps for the beginner – see **9**.

782 Shutter-priority
Buy a shutter-priority automatic if you expect to do plenty of sports and action photography, so that you can set a faster shutter speed to freeze movement properly.

783 Aperture-priority
An aperture-priority exposure system is better than a shutter-priority (**782**) if you need full control over depth of field for subjects such as portraits.

784 Multi mode exposure
Multi mode cameras give you the luxury of choosing the exposure mode to suit the situation. So if you want to shoot many different types of subject, the multi mode will give you the best of all worlds. But before you pay out the extra for a multi mode camera, ask yourself if you really need this many modes. Most photographers find that they use only one mode 95% of the time. Provided you have manual override, a shutter- or aperture-priority model will do as well.

785 TTL flash metering
If you plan to do plenty of flash photography, consider buying one of the more expensive 35mm SLRs with an off-the-film flash metering facility. This saves any problems compensating for filters and other lens attachments when using flash.

786 Depth of field preview
Make sure the SLR you buy has a depth of field preview button (**176–177**) – it is essential for serious photography. Some more recent SLRs have dispensed with it – yet without it, you cannot stop the lens down to the taking aperture to assess the depth of field visually and see whether the right parts of the picture are sharp.

787 Shots in the dark
If you expect to take a lot of pictures in dim light, choose a camera in which the glowing LED (light-emitting diode) viewfinder display is readable in the dark. Some cameras have red lights that glow alongside a scale lit by daylight – in darkness, you can see the light but not the scale. So you need a camera in which the LED is behind a cut-out, so that you see the shutter speed set glowing brightly.

788 Changing finders
If you want a really versatile 35mm SLR, go for one that accepts interchangeable viewfinders. You can, for instance, fit an action finder, ideal for situations where you cannot get your eye right up against the camera eyepiece. See also **180–193**.

Action finder

789
Beware of so-called full information viewfinders – the only really vital information you need is (1) aperture, (2) shutter speed, (3) under-/overexposure warning. A flash ready signal is optional, but useful. Any extra flashing lights or bleeps are simply distractions.

790
Don't assume that a camera's auto exposure control can give correct exposures up to a few minutes. No camera can compensate for the fact that the sensitivity of film drops dramatically when exposure time exceeds 1 sec – see end of tip 648. The result is that even if the camera is working perfectly, your exposures will be underexposed with time exposures unless you compensate.

791
Beware when buying a 'grey import' – that is, a camera which was not imported through the maker's appointed agent. You may not be covered properly against faulty equipment. Check the guarantee carefully.

792
Don't be persuaded to buy a camera simply because it will stand up to hard wear better. Unless you use your camera professionally, you are unlikely ever to wear it out, whatever make you buy. Even if you go mountaineering, it is probably better to buy a cheaper camera, insure it fully, and replace it when it gets damaged.

793 Fast shutter
A 35mm SLR feature well worth looking for if you are keen on sports action shots is a shutter speed of 1/2000 or faster. All the top-of-the-range 'pro' models have this feature, but so too do a number aimed more at the amateur market, such as the Nikon FM2 – which actually gives 1/4000 as well. However, if you don't have a real penchant for action shots, you will rarely use these speeds.

794 Data days
If you have a new baby or a growing family, consider buying one of the newer cameras, like the Minolta X-700, that has a databack as standard. The databack will print the date and other information about the shot on every frame of the film, so when you look at the photos in later years, you'll never have to say, 'I wonder how old she was when we took that . . .?' Databacks are also a handy way of recording information for the nature photographer.

1 3 83

795 Spot on
One of the traditional problems with TTL metering in SLRs is the way it can be misled by some subjects (see **142–145**). If you cannot be bothered with a hand-held meter, but want at least some of its accuracy – perhaps for landscape photography – buy one of the new

cameras that give computerized spot light readings over the whole frame as well as the conventional centre-weighted reading.

796 Sharp ears
For some people the process of squinting into the viewfinder to focus the image is part of the joy of SLR photography (**5, 187**); to others it is just tedious. If your sympathies are with them, consider buying one of the 35mm SLRs that make focusing so easy you hardly have to look at all. Sharp focus is indicated by a little green light, or even an audible bleep – but remember these only work properly when the subject is positioned in certain ways – see **43**.

797 Sync-in fast
If you expect to use flash frequently – especially for fill-in (see **286**) – yet want neither the expense nor the bother of a rollfilm SLR, look for a 35mm SLR (such as the Nikon FM2) which gives a reasonably fast flash synchronization speed.

798 Snapshot SLRs
You can combine the versatility of 35mm SLR photography with the simple, no-fuss compact approach by buying a 35mm SLR with fully automatic 'programmed' exposure. With programmed exposure, both aperture and shutter speed are set completely automatically – you literally point, focus and shoot. In the Canon T50, even the film is wound on automatically. However, it is important to fully appreciate that you have no control over exposure at all, except by altering the film speed dial.

799 Buying secondhand
If you cannot afford the type of camera you feel you really need, think about buying secondhand. With so many startling technical advances every year, cameras are quickly rendered obsolete and resale values are generally poor. So provided you are willing to put up with last year's model, you can often pick up genuine bargains by buying secondhand. See 800–808.

800 Solid quality
When you're buying secondhand, go for a basic high-quality camera rather than one with a host of automatic features. Although modern automatic and semi-automatic cameras are remarkably reliable, there is simply more to go wrong – and if anything does go wrong, the chances are that repair will be prohibitively expensive.

801 Private or shop?
Buy from a dealer rather than privately unless you are sure of the camera's soundness. You are unlikely to pick up a real bargain at a dealer, but the chances are that you will get a good, reliable camera – you may even be able to get a written guarantee.

802 Is it all there?
Before you buy, make sure that none of the essential extras (lens cap and so on) are lost.

803 Pre-purchase check
Check that all the camera controls are functioning properly. The focus and aperture rings should turn smoothly without sticking through their full range. The shutter should fire perfectly at every shutter speed. And there should be no slackness in the wind-on lever or the lens mount.

804
You can check the operation of a camera's iris/diaphragm by setting the aperture to f16 and the shutter to one second. Then open the camera back and press the shutter release. If you look through the lens, you should see the iris blades close to a small hole without hesitation.

805
You can check the flash synchronization if you fit a hot-shoe flash unit. Set the lens to full aperture and the shutter to the maximum flash synchronization speed. Then open the camera back and look through the lens while you point the camera (and flash) at a white wall. You should see the whole frame brilliantly illuminated. If it is completely dark, or if only part of the frame is bright, the flash is not synchronizing correctly.

806
If you can borrow a friend's camera or light meter, you can check the accuracy of the meter of the camera you're buying by comparing readings for different subjects.

807
Don't buy a used camera if there are any signs that it has been dropped. Look for dents or any signs of buckling on the bodywork – particularly on the front of the camera. The camera's controls may still function perfectly, but a minute gap may mean the body is not lightproof.

808
Beware of amateur 'repairs'. Most amateur attempts to fix a camera usually succeed only in doing more damage. Evidence of damage or burring on the tiny screw heads should not be taken lightly.

809
Don't bother to buy an expensive rangefinder camera if you only expect to take pictures outdoors in fine weather. Really accurate focusing is only needed in dim light when you are obliged to set the camera to its widest aperture (see **172**). At the narrow apertures used outdoors, cheaper 'guesstimate' focused camers are perfectly adequate.

810
Don't assume a camera can take pictures in any lighting conditions if it has a built-in flash. The small flash units built in to most compacts will only illuminate subjects fairly close to the camera.

811 Basic 35mm compact
If you want a 35mm compact (**24**) for a complete beginner (**25**), particularly for a child, get a basic model with a minimum of functions. A fixed-focus camera, or one that uses symbols for focusing, is ideal – anything more will be wasted. If you can afford it, get a camera with fully automatic exposure – it is barely more vulnerable to damage than simpler models and will give the budding photographer more scope. See also **24–31**.

812 Mouldings
When you're buying a camera for a child or for snapshots on the beach, look for a camera with a strong, neat, moulded plastic body. If the corners are rounded and all the controls and the lens are well recessed into the body moulding – as on the Canon Snappy and the Cosina CX-5 – the camera will not be completely proof against damage, but should take rough handling well.

813 Easy loading
Many people find loading difficult, so an easy-loading mechanism is worthwhile.

814 Baby photos
If you want to take pictures of a new baby, make sure that the 35mm compact will focus on subjects about 3ft (1m) or closer to the camera – you need to be able to get this close to fill the frame with your tiny subject.

815 Autofocus
The 35mm compact with an autofocus facility is perfect if

you want to shoot a wide range of subjects with a minimum of fuss and bother. But before buying an autofocus camera, make sure that it will operate in dim light. It is in dim light that autofocus really comes into its own – because focusing by any other means is usually difficult, or impossible. The autofocus is therefore ideal for taking pictures at a dimly lit party, or in a night club. In bright light, focusing is in any case not so critical because narrower apertures can be used (**172**). Cameras using the 'active infra-red' system, such as the Canon AF35, will focus in complete darkness.

816 Top pocket
A few cameras at the top of the price range, such as the Minox and the Olympus XA, use the full 35mm negative size (see **47**) and are really no bigger than a cigarette packet. Although expensive, they give results that match many 35mm SLRs and they are genuine pocket cameras, smaller than some 110s. For the experienced photographer who wants a camera at the ready all the time, either as a supplement to an SLR, or as a prime camera, they are ideal.

817 Disc or 110?

For sheer simplicity of operation, disc cameras are hard to
beat – even the flash goes off
automatically to ensure that no
pictures within range are
underexposed. The flat, rigid
film also means that they give
slightly sharper pictures than a
110. And they are so thin that
they will slip even into a shirt
pocket. See also 11–21.

818

If you think you may take
plenty of pictures, buy a
pocket 110 rather than a disc
camera. Disc cameras are not
only more expensive to buy,
they are also more expensive
to run because they only give
15 frames on each disc.

819 Weather symbols

With such a small frame size,
the most basic pocket 110s will
only give acceptable contrast
and colour rendition when well
exposed. So go for a 110 that
has some exposure control,
such as weather symbols, or
for one with automatic
exposure.

Bright sun   Hazy sun   Cloudy   Flash

820 Smooth shutter

It is worth paying a little extra to
get a camera with a sensitive
shutter release – the 110 format
is very prone to camera shake
and if you have to press hard to
operate the shutter, you can
easily jog the camera. Because
of the location of the shutter
release, disc cameras are
slightly less vulnerable to
shake than 110s.

821 Rollfilm cameras

For sheer technical quality, a
'medium format', rollfilm
camera is hard to beat However, they are expensive to
buy and run (see 46–48).
Unless you are certain you will
use a rollfilm camera extensively, hire one when you need
it, rather than buying outright –
many professionals do the
same. See also 44 and 822.

822

If you do decide to buy a
rollfilm camera, hire out as
many models as possible
beforehand to find out which
suits your way of working best.

823

When working out the cost of a
rollfilm camera, remember
that you will almost certainly
need a quality tripod and other
essential items.

824

The various parts of an SLR
rollfilm camera are usually
sold separately. So if you see a
low price quoted, it will probably be for the body alone. You
will still have to buy the film
back and the lens – each of
which may cost more than the
body.

825 Leaf or focal plane?

If you are short of money, buy a
rollfilm SLR that has focal plane
shutter (always sited in the
camera body) rather than leaf
shutters in the lenses. This way
you only buy one shutter. The
leaf shutter is an integral part of
the lens, and each time you
buy a new lens, you also pay
for a new shutter – extremely
expensive.

826
Beware of free gifts.
Dealers that offer
free colour
processing with the
camera you buy
could simply be
trying to ensure you
buy most of your film
from them too. 'Free'
film and processing
are widely
available. See 74.

827
Think before buying
a disc camera if you
want to project your
pictures on a screen.
Slide films are hard
to get for these ·
cameras. For the 110
format, however, a
Kodachrome slide
film is available
widely from Kodak
stockists.

828
Don't feel restricted to the currently available models if you want to try rollfilm photography. Initially, you will not need much in the way of technology. Look around camera dealers for secondhand alternatives. Stick to the brand names you know – some of the obscure names may be of dubious quality.

829
Don't forget that if you are upgrading from 35mm, most of your accessories, including filters and perhaps even your camera bag, will be unusable with a rollfilm camera. These items too must be included in the cost of the new camera.

830 Synchronization
If you use fill-in flash frequently (**286–289**), and you are considering buying a rollfilm SLR, it could be worth paying extra for one that can be fitted with leaf shutter lenses. Such cameras synchronize with flash at many shutter speeds.

831 Back-up
Check that the rollfilm camera you buy can be fitted with a Polaroid back. This facility, which allows you to make test shots on instant film, is one of the most valuable features of the larger format cameras – though Polaroid backs are also available for top professional 35mm cameras, and Polaroid have introduced an 'instant' 35mm slide film. See also **37**.

832 Formats
Rollfilm cameras all use 120 film, but there are a number of different negative formats – 6 × 4.5cm (used by Mamiyas and Bronicas), 6 × 6cm (Hasselblads, Bronica, Rollei and Yashica) and 6 × 7cm (Mamiya, Pentax and Plaubel). The square (6 × 6cm) format is the most popular, but if you have graduated from 35mm, you will find the similarly shaped 6 × 4.5cm easiest to work with.

833
The Hasselblad is the supreme rollfilm camera, but if you want a 6 × 6cm format SLR, the Bronica SQ offers high quality at barely half the price.

834 Portability
If you want a rollfilm camera, but don't want to be restricted to using the camera on a

tripod (as is generally the case with the rollfilm SLR), consider buying one of the lightweight direct vision models: the Plaubel or the Fujica. They will not accept Polaroid backs (**37**, **831**), but the Fujica is no heavier than the Nikon F3, and a rangefinder aids focusing on both cameras.

835 TLRS
If you want to get into the rollfilm format cheaply, buy a used twin lens reflex (TLR). TLRS (**45**) used to be popular with professionals, but have fallen out of favour, so there are many quality TLRS to be found at bargain prices.

836 Amphibious
For fun pictures in the swimming pool, or of the family splashing in the sea, all you need is a simple weatherproof 110 camera, like the Minolta Weathermatic or the Hanimex Amphibian. These cameras will not give 35mm quality, but they are ideal for snapshots on the beach. You can drop them on a towel with little fear of damage by salt or sand, and you can take them swimming.

837 Plastic bag
If you own an ordinary SLR with a wide-angle lens, you can take up underwater photography cheaply by buying an EWA bag. An EWA bag is simply a transparent plastic bag with a rigid porthole. For underwater shots (but see **838**) you simply seal your camera in the bag and operate it in the normal way with an internal glove. Some find them awkward to use, but they are inexpensive and compact. See also **839**.

838 Deep down

For shots at a depth of more than 30ft (10m), you can hire a purpose-built camera or a rigid housing for a few days – long periods are likely to be prohibitively costly.

839 Nikonos

If you are a keen scuba diver, consider buying a Nikonos underwater camera instead of a conventional SLR. Although it has a direct vision viewfinder, the Nikonos has many of the facilities of the SLR, including a range of interchangeable lenses. Not all of the lenses can be used out of the water, but otherwise the camera is as effective on land as it is in the sea. See also 837–838.

840 Panoramas

The cheapest way to shoot panoramas is to take a se-quence of shots with an or-dinary camera placed on a tripod. But if you want to specialize in panoramas it may be worth buying a Wide-lux or a Globuscope.

841 Stereo pictures

You can make a stereo pair of pictures of static subjects for a 3D effect without any special equipment, simply by taking two separate shots, moving the camera sideways 6cm be-tween shots. But if you want to make stereo photography a lit-tle easier – especially if you want to shoot moving subjects – buy a stereo beamsplitter at-tachment. See also 842–843.

842

For the real stereo enthusiast, there are special stereo cameras to be found. Few are made nowadays, but you can sometimes pick up an old Iloca from the 50s at a bargain price.

843 3D prints

Stereo images need special viewing apparatus, but you can get 3D prints to hand around just like normal snaps with the Nimslo camera system. The Nimslo camera has four separate lenses giving four half-frame negatives, each showing a slightly dif-ferent view, every time you press the shutter. These are then combined in the process-ing lab in microscopic strips on a single print.

844

Don't buy an EWA bag if you want to dive below 30ft (10m) – the pressure at depths greater than this will usually create a leak.

845

A specialist camera is for specialists – unless you intend to do a lot of the particular type of work, **don't** buy one. Remember, most of the effects possible with specialist cameras such as stereo and panoramas can be improvised on normal cameras.

846
Don't ignore the less glamorous accessories when you're building up your photographic outfit. Items such as blower brushes and lens cleaning tissues are just as important as motor drives and meters.

847
Don't assume that photographic shops are the only places to buy your photographic accessories. Some of the most useful of all extras are to be found in hardware, stationery and other shops. When you're in a specialist hardware store, for instance, keep an eye open for useful items like gaffer tape – and see **740, 745, 747** and **760**.

848 Accessories
Before you buy any accessory, think first – do you really need it? Photography is about pictures, not equipment. See also **776**.

849 Hand-held meter
For really accurate exposure, get a hand-held meter, even if you have a good TTL meter in your camera. With a hand-held meter, not only is it easier to get good readings from specific areas of the subject, but you can also take 'incident' light readings (**147**) – readings of the light actually falling on the subject. See also **850–851**.

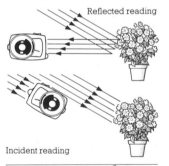

Reflected reading

Incident reading

850 Selenium cell meter
If you want a hand-held meter to complement your TTL meter, get the selenium cell type. These have a limited sensitivity range and become less accurate with age, but they need no batteries, they are durable and, above all, they are much cheaper than other types of meter. See also **849, 851, 748**.

851
If you want a selenium cell meter (**850**), think about buying secondhand – the Weston Master is a classic.

852 CdS and SPD meters
If you plan to do plenty of night photography, it might be worth investing in cadmium sulphide (CdS) or a silicon photodiode (SPD) meter – preferably an SPD because fewer and fewer CdS meters are manufactured. Both types are expensive, but they are extremely sensitive, typically giving readings in light as dim as − 2EV or even − 8EV on some models. (EVs, Exposure Values, are simply a measure of the shutter speed and aperture combination needed to give correct exposure with 100 ISO film, not allowing for reciprocity failure – see end of tip **648**. Most TTL meters on most SLRs will read only down to − 1EV – that is, 1 sec at f1.4. See also **853**.

CdS   SPD

853 Meter displays
If you buy an SPD meter for shots at night, make sure that the reading is given on a glowing digital LED (light-emitting diode) display system. See also **854**.

854
Although an analog meter display (**853**) is better for painstaking precision exposure and quick assessment of contrast, digital display meters are much easier to use and usually have a useful memory facility.

855 Flash and colour
Some meters, such as the Calcuflash and the Vivitar LX range, can meter both flash and available light at the same time. If you do much studio work, use one of these – or a meter such as the Gossen Profisix, which can be converted into a colour temperature or flash meter.

856 Enlarging
If you do much darkroom work, you can save yourself a little money by getting an attachment for a hand meter that takes exposure readings for enlarging rather than a separate enlarging meter. Only a few meters accept these attachments, so make sure you get the right one.

857 Spot meters
Spot meters give the most accurate exposure metering of all – taking a reading from a small spot in the subject, perhaps over an angle of view of only one degree. But they are difficult to use effectively and can be very expensive.

858 Diffusion cap
If you want to make incident light readings (147) frequently but cannot afford a separate hand meter, buy a translucent dome lens cap.

859 Film drives
If you want to buy a motorized film transport, perhaps for sports shots or studio portrait sessions, buy an autowind rather than a motor drive. An autowind will not give the same prodigious framing rate, nor will it fire the shutter for you. But it is generally much cheaper to buy, infinitely cheaper to run and, most important, allows you to choose the moment you fire the shutter. See 862.

Autowind

860 Eye cups
A rubber cup that fits on to the eyepiece of your camera makes viewfinding more comfortable and shades the eyepiece so that it is easier to see the focusing screen. For people who wear glasses, the last is an especially important point: distancing the camera from the eye makes the focusing screen image that much less bright and contrasty. See also 205.

861 A1 penknife
Buy yourself a Swiss Army knife to stow away in your bag – it could be invaluable.

862
Don't be led astray by the exciting whirr of a motor drive – it will not make your pictures any more exciting or dynamic. All a motor drive will do unless handled properly is eat film. There are situations where a motor drive is useful – for taking a series of exposures as the sun sinks below the horizon, for instance, or when you are operating the camera by remote control. But be sure you will take advantage of these benefits before you pay out for an expensive motor drive. See also 542, 859 and 863.

863
Beware: autowinds and motor drives are not the same things. An autowind is usually much cheaper and lighter, but it will not advance the film at anything like the rate of a powerful motordrive, nor will it fire the shutter automatically. If the ad specifies a 'motorized film advance', it probably means an autowind not a motor drive. See 859, 862.

864
Don't buy extra lenses just for the sake of it. A new lens will not make you a better photographer. Remember, you can take exactly the same pictures on a standard lens as you can on a telephoto lens, simply by cropping the finished photo. All a telephoto offers is increased quality and convenience for certain shots. See also **865.**

865
Don't bother to buy an expensive telephoto if you never enlarge your pictures beyond postcard size.

866 Standard practice
Most photographers automatically buy a standard 50mm lens with their camera body, but it is well worth considering the alternatives. If you are fairly experienced, a wide-angle lens might prove more versatile – you can be sure of getting everything you want in the frame, then cropping to get the right composition at the printing stage. See **890.** If you are just starting, however, a telephoto, or even a telephoto zoom, might make a good first lens because it simplifies composition.

867 Planning
Before you buy any new lens, try to work out just how your system will develop. A 135mm telephoto, for instance, is the ideal compromise between a 105mm and a 200mm, and, if you never get another medium telephoto, it is a good lens to have. But if you subsequently decide to buy either of the alternatives, it will become redundant.

868 Systems lenses
For a neat, uniform camera system, with a high resale value, buy a lens made by the same manufacturer as your camera.

869 Independents
If your budget is limited, have a look at alternative lenses available from the independent manufacturers.

870 Cheap lenses
Quality is variable at the bottom end of the lens market, and it is generally best to avoid cheap wide-angle lenses. Wide-angles are optically complex and any cost-cutting may reduce quality significantly. Zoom lenses suffer in the same way.

871 Test roll
Unless you are absolutely sure of a lens's quality, ask the dealer if you can shoot off a roll of film with it before buying. If you use Ektachrome, you can in many places have it processed and examine the results the same day. Look particularly for signs of darkening round the edges of the frame (vignetting), colour fringes (chromatic aberration), distortion of straight lines and general lack of sharpness and contrast. If any of these seem excessive, don't buy the lens.

872 Lens mount
If you buy a lens made by one of the independents, make sure it has the right lens mount to fit your camera. You can buy adaptors for most makes of camera, but this adds to the price and makes the lens more awkward to use.

873 Focusing ring
On some lenses you turn the focusing ring clockwise to focus closer; on others, you turn it anticlockwise. Make sure all the lenses you buy focus the same way.

874 Filter size

When you're thinking of buy-ing an extra lens, look at the size of filter it takes. If it is dif-ferent from the lenses you already own, you will have to buy either a stepping ring or a new set of filters. If the filters are large, this could be expensive.

875 Teleconverters

Teleconverters are a cheap way of getting longer focal lengths, but it is worth paying a little extra for a good-quality converter – with the poorer converters, picture quality will often be worse than you would get by simply enlarging the desired area of a picture taken on the unconverted lens. See **340–348**.

876 Steady teles

If you buy a long telephoto, make sure it has a tripod socket.

877 Follow focus

If you want a long telephoto for sports photography where you have to keep a fast-moving subject in focus, think about getting a lens with a rapid focus facility such as the Novoflex RFF with its pistol grip focusing. Or, if you have a lot of money to spend, a telephoto with inter-nal focusing is worthwhile.

878 Closest focusing

Most 300mm lenses will focus down to 11½ft (3.5m); some focus as close as 4½ft (1.4m). So if you want a long telephoto for wildlife – for close-ups of but-terflies on flowers, say – it is worth looking for a lens that will focus close. See also **347**.

879 Preset diaphragm

If you want a long telephoto for landscape work with an SLR, a lens with a manually preset diaphragm is a good buy. You will have to stop down (see **176**) manually before each shot, but this short delay hardly signi-fies in landscape work. And the simple construction of lenses with manually preset diaphragms means you can buy good quality for a reasonable outlay. (The dia-phragm is the assembly of metal leaves which creates the adjustable aperture – see **168**, **170**).

880 Automatic diaphragm

For subjects where timing is crucial an automatic dia-phragm is a must on an SLR. The diaphragm, controlling the aperture size, stops down automatically to the 'taking' aperture (see **176**) as you press the shutter release. (See **168** and **170** for an explanation of aperture.)

881 Pincushion distortion

Before you buy a long tele-photo, check for 'pincushion' distortion. Look through the viewfinder with the lens in place at a strong vertical line, such as the edge of a wall. Swing the camera slowly past this edge. If the edge appears to bow when at the edge of the focusing screen, the lens has pincushion distortion.

882 Mirror lenses

Some of the cheaper 300mm mirror lenses are barely big-ger than a standard (for 35mm cameras) and may weigh and cost even less. See also **320–323**.

883

Don't think that the small size and low weight of a mirror lens means that it can be used for hand-held shots at shutter speeds of less than 1/500 sec – the long focal length and low inertia can mean camera shake is just as much a problem as with telephotos. The advantage of the mirror lens's compactness lies in is portability.

884

Think twice about buying a mirror lens if you want a long lens for bringing foreground objects such as butterflies or small birds closer. Even if it focuses sufficiently closely, you will probably find the depth of field far too restricted to get your subject sharp. And because mirrors have a fixed aperture, you cannot even stop down to increase the depth of field. If you want a long lens for this type of shot, buy a telephoto.

BUYING LENSES

885
Beware of lenses with a smaller maximum aperture than average – that is, very slow lenses. A slow telephoto will have to be used on a tripod in all but the very brightest conditions. A slow wide-angle lens cannot be opened wide enough to allow you to focus selectively. See **886**.

886
Beware also of paying a great deal extra for a lens that is only a fraction of a stop faster. A lens really needs to be substantially faster to be worth paying extra for. See **887**.

887
Don't buy a super-fast lens unless you are absolutely sure you will take advantage of the extra aperture. Unless you buy a very expensive 'aspheric element' lens, you will not only find the super-fast a great deal more bulky, but it may also give slightly inferior results to a slower lens at comparable apertures. Only when you take pictures at maximum aperture will its advantages really show up.

888 Long shots
Buy a mirror telescope designed for astronomy (the Celestron range is excellent) if you want ultra-long focal lengths for a relatively modest outlay. With a T2 adaptor and an inverter, you can fit one of these astronomical telescopes to virtually any SLR. Focal lengths of up to 2,000, even 3,000mm are common. See also **889**.

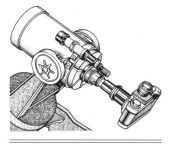

889 Binoculars
If you own a pair of binoculars, use them as a cheap alternative to a long telehoto simply by holding one eyepiece firmly to the camera lens.

890 Wide-angle
A 35mm wide-angle makes a useful alternative to a standard lens. It gives natural perspective, it's not too wide for full flash coverage and it is generally the cheapest wide-angle in a given range.

891 24 or 28mm?
Buy a 28mm if your budget is limited – the same quality or speed in a 24mm costs more.

892 Budget wide-angles
If you decide to buy a budget wide-angle lens, check it first – see **893**.

893
If a wide-angle makes the horizon bow unduly (see **892**) as you move the camera up and down, the lens is suffering from barrel distortion.

894 Zoom lenses
If you are buying a zoom lens to save carrying a range of alternative fixed-focus lenses, make sure you get a small compact zoom, or the weight and space saving will be lost.

35mm
85mm
50mm
35–85mm zoom

895 Taking steps
Before you go out and buy a mid-range zoom, bear in mind that you might be able to get the framing you want with a medium telephoto simply by walking – and the medium telephoto will give you better quality for the money.

896 Matched multiplier
If you plan to use supplementary lenses to increase the focal length of a zoom lens, buy a zoom with a matched multiplier – quality will be substantially better.

897 Variable focus
When you're buying a zoom for rapid framing changes, such as you might need in sports photography, make sure you get a true zoom, not a varifocus lens. Varifocus lenses have to be refocused every time you change the focal length.

898 Reversing rings

The simplest and cheapest way of getting in close is to buy a reversing ring which allows you to attach the standard lens back-to-front. Typically, a 50mm lens then focuses on a subject at 5in (12.5cm). But without bellows, you cannot focus at any other distance. And the aperture-metering connections will not work.

899 Supplementary lenses

Even if your camera does not take interchangeable lenses, you can take close-ups by fitting a supplementary lens over the front of the prime lens. The magnifying power of a supplementary lens is given in *dioptres*, which are a measure of the lens's focal length divided into 1m. But unless you stop right down (see 170 and 179), definition is poor.

900 Extension tubes

If you want to take quality close-ups but cannot afford special equipment, buy a set of extension tubes. These are simple tubes inserted between the camera body and the prime lens, allowing considerable freedom to focus on close subjects. With a single tube you can focus on a range of subject distances; a set of three increases the versatility.

901 Combinations

Use extension tubes (900) in combination to extend their range. With a set of three, a fourth extra extension distance is achieved by combining all three.

902 Macro

If you expect to do much close-up work, think about buying a macro instead of a standard lens. Macros are easy to use for close-ups and give high-quality images. And, even at infinity, image quality as nearly as good as with a standard. But macros are twice the price, and have smaller maximum apertures. See 903, 906, 907.

903 Stamp album

For shots of small, flat objects like stamps, you need a macro lens. Extension tubes and reversing rings do not focus properly at this range over the whole frame.

904 Bellows

For utmost versatility and top quality with very close subjects – that is, true 'macro' (larger-than-life) subjects – bellows are the answer. Those made by the camera manufacturer can be expensive, but cheaper, independently made sets are usually adequate. See also 905.

905 Manual or auto?

If you will only use bellows occasionally, buy the cheaper manual bellows. Only if you use bellows extensively is it worth paying for bellows which stop down (176) automatically before a shot. See also 904.

906

Don't be confused by the term 'micro' (as in Micro Nikkor and the names of some other lenses). It simply means the lens is a macro.

907

Don't expect the macro facility available on some zoom lenses to give the same quality as a genuine macro lens. It is a useful additional feature for the photographer who wants to shoot a wide range of subjects with a single lens. But it is rarely suitable for critical close-up photography.

908

Don't assume a split-field close-up lens will work every time you want to combine a close foreground with a distant background. A split-field attachment is a supplementary close-up lens cut in half, so one half of the picture can be focused on a close subject, while the other is focused at infinity. But this only works well if the subject happens to split neatly across the centre of the frame.

909
Don't be misled by claims that some filters will impair the image quality significantly, but see **913**. Every major filter manufacturer produces filters that could degrade the image slightly – but the effect is so small that it is barely detectable even under a microscope. You can certainly disregard this factor for all normal photographic purposes. Filters only really start to have a detrimental effect on the image when they become scratched, or you use them in combination – see **356**. Only the expensive gelatin filters are noticeably superior optically – but you would have to be doing very critical work to appreciate it.

910 Filter choice
Glass filters are by far the best type to buy for regular use because they are robust and easy to handle – your skylight, 81A and polarizing filters especially should be of this type. But see **911–913**.

911
For special effects or filters you use only occasionally, the square rigid plastic 'system' filters (see **916**) are more economical than glass filters. Plastic graduated filters are particularly useful because you can move the filter around in its mount to get just the right effect.

912
If you want the widest possible range and the best quality, thin gelatin or 'gel' filters, such as those made by Kodak, are the answer. But they are expensive and very vulnerable to damage; they are really filters for the professional.

913 Polarizers
For the best results, get a circular filter made by your camera manufacturer or by a quality independent brand such as Hoya or B&W – some square filters and the cheaper circular polarizers may be less satisfactory.

Circular polarizer

914 Wide angle problems
If you have a wide-angle lens with such a deeply curved front element that you cannot fit filters, buy a gelatin filter and tape it over the rear of the lens (cut to fit in the lens mount). See also **915**.

915
Buy special 'extra large' filters to prevent vignetting with ultra-wide-angle lenses. These filters are much bigger than the front element of the lens but have a similar thread size.

916 System filters
Some cameras and lenses – and particularly rollfilm cameras – require very large filters and these can be extremely expensive. To reduce your costs, buy into a 'system' of filters using a single holder that accepts a range of square plastic filters.

Cokin 'system' filter holder and square slot-in filter

917 Large but cheap
If you can't afford the giant filters needed to go over the large front element of a fast telephoto lens, get gelatin filters and tape them over the much smaller rear element of the lens (see **914**).

918 After-effects?
Think carefully before buying a whole range of special-effects filters. Ask yourself how often you'll use them. Some find they use such devices only a couple of times before the novelty wears off. One of the joys of photography is achieving a variety of pictures, but some of the more spectacular special-effects devices simply give many versions of the same picture. It may be wise to buy say a couple of the most subtle, versatile filters to start with, such as a graduated filter and a starburst. If you do want one of the more outlandish effects, experiment with making it yourself: it is easy to cut all kinds of shapes into silver foil discs and fit them into a filter holder.

919 Filter wallets
To store glass and plastic filters safely and accessibly in your camera bag, buy a filter wallet, but see 921. You can slip each filter in and out of an individual pocket as desired without the bother of screwing and unscrewing drum boxes. See also 920, 349.

920 Filter roll
If you have a number of round glass filters, buy metal end caps. These are like metal filters – you screw all your filters of the same size into a

roll, then put the caps on either end. When you want to use a filter, simply break the roll at the appropriate place. See also 919, 349.

921 Storing gels
Gelatin filters (912) are extremely delicate and easily damaged, so buy a special gelatin filter holder to store them in. This keeps the filter flat and protects it from scratches.

922 Rubber lenshood
For photographing in confined spaces, such as crowds, get a collapsible rubber lenshood which will fold back out of the way when not in use. It will also protect the rim of the lens from knocks.

923 Deep hood
For proper shading of a long telephoto lens, you need a deep metal hood built specially for the lens. A proper hood will make a surprising amount of difference to contrast levels in your shots – but make sure the hood shades the lens properly from stray light without causing vignetting. See 310.

924 Bellows hoods
If you want the most versatile possible hood, buy a bellows type hood. The hood will give you complete control over shading, and you can use the same hood on a wide variety of lenses. Unfortunately, they are rather fragile and bulky and so are difficult to carry around. They are really professional studio equipment and you should only buy them if you do plenty of studio work.

925
Don't forget to check the thread size of a new filter fits all the lenses on which you wish to use it. If all the lenses have different thread sizes, don't buy five different sizes of the same filter. Buy one plastic 'system' filter, plus the universal holder, and mounting rings for each different lens: much more economical.

926
Don't miss out on using film of varying speeds to suit lighting conditions; see **61–65.** Modern fast films especially increase the scope of most cameras in a dramatic fashion.

927 Bulk buy
If you can afford it, buy all your film in packets of ten or more – but make sure that each roll has the same emulsion batch number marked on the packet. Not only will this save you money, but you can be sure that each roll will have identical colour characteristics and speed. See also **928.**

928 Iced rolls
If you buy film in bulk, store it in the fridge immediately after purchase. It will remain usable way past the nominal expiry date and each roll should retain its original colour and speed characteristics.

929 Fast colour
For low light colour shots, and for colour shots with long lenses in less than favourable light, use one of the new generation of colour films such as Kodak's VR 1000, which actually gives superor quality to the 400 ISO film it supersedes. These are such remarkable films, in fact, that no one should miss trying them.

930 Fast monochrome
If you want relatively grain-free black and white shots in dim light, use one of the chromogenic films such as XP1. Because like colour film they use dyes to form the image rather than grains of silver as in conventional monochrome films, they suffer noticeably less from grain when pushed to high speeds. See **84.**

931 In the grain
For grainy, atmospheric effects, use Kodak Recording film rated at 1600 ISO for black and white, and a 1000 ISO film like 3M's for colour.

932 Giant monochrome
For mural-sized black and white enlargements from 35mm film use Kodak Technical Pan Film. It gives such good definition that any fault visible in the print is more likely to be caused by the camera or enlarger lenses. But to get normal contrast you must use a specially formulated developer.

933 Instant slides
If you want 'instant' slides, or you want to make Polaroid test shots on a normal 35mm camera, buy a roll of Polaroid's 35mm film and their special processor. It will give you high-definition slides, completely dry, in a matter of minutes.

934 Tungsten speed
For shots in poor artificial light, such as urban street lighting, try 3M's 640T. It is a fast colour film balanced for tungsten light.

935 In a strange light
For fascinating distorted colour effects, use infra-red colour film. It is mainly used for special technical purposes such as crop surveys, but there is no reason why you can't use it for weird colour shots.

936 Slide copies
For high-quality copies of slides, get Kodak's special duplicating film, now available in 36-exposure rolls for both daylight and tungsten use.

937 Remember
If you expect to buy new lenses and accessories, buy a bag or case that will hold all of your outfit rather than an ever-ready case. An ever-ready case will simply get in the way – you will find a camera bag or case much more useful. But get a neckstrap to hold the camera in tricky situations. See also 391.

938 Fishing bags
Soft bags designed originally for hunting and fishing can be ideal for carrying your camera gear – they are strong, light and inconspicuous (see 402).

939 Waterproof
A camera bag should protect your equipment against even the heaviest downpours. It must also keep out sand and dust. See also 740, 756, 760.

940 Stitched up
When buying a camera bag, always examine the stitching closely – look particularly at the places where straps and handles are attached.

941 Internal protection
For proper protection, a soft bag should have a reinforced base and compartments made from foam – preferably solid cell foam, not open cell foam – for each major item of your equipment.

942 Alloy cases
For ultimate protection, buy an alloy case. They are much less comfortable to carry around than soft bags, but they should protect your equipment against all but the hardest knocks. And you can stand on them to shoot over the heads of a crowd; or sit on them when they become too heavy to carry. See also 947.

943 Packed case
If an alloy case contains foam that has to be cut and shaped into compartments for your equipment, keep the compartments well apart. Cramming in too much lessens the cushioning against shocks.

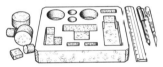

944 Special cases
Insulated bags such as the one sold with Kodak's trademark on it have their use for carrying film in hot climates – see 750. Purpose-made tripod bags may be less useful. Small tripods pack easily into suitcases; large tripods need robust protection, such as a golf bag. See 626.

945 Second bag
If you own a large case or bag, it is usually worth buying a smaller, lightweight soft bag for carrying just a few items when you have to be mobile. It need not be anything elaborate – a cheap army surplus canvas bag is adequate. But make sure it can be fastened securely – a zip is best.

946
Don't try to save money by buying a very cheap camera bag. The chances are that it will not give expensive photographic equipment the protection it needs. Nor will it last long – and straps could break at the worst possible time.

947
Beware: many 'alloy' camera cases, particularly at the cheap end of the market, are not alloy at all; they are simply wooden cases with a thin skin of embossed aluminium. These are fine for storing equipment at home, but they are not ideal for travelling. A solid alloy case with rubber gaskets to keep out moisture is a much better bet. See also 942.

948
Don't try to use a lightweight tripod designed for small 35mm cameras with a rollfilm camera.

949
Be extra careful if you ever trust your camera to one of the supports that depend on rubber suckers to hold your camera to a glass window. They work most of the time but might slip at a crucial moment.

950
Don't rely on a plastic clamp if you want to attach your camera to something. Use a G-clamp (C-clamp) designed for woodwork, with a ¼in (6mm) bolt welded securely to one side – the bolt will screw into the camera's tripod socket.

951
Don't forget you can often improvise effective camera support – see 116–119.

952 Heavy metal
If you want complete stability, go for the heaviest tripod you can afford – weight is everything in tripods, and no tripod, no matter how well designed, will give you a really firm base if it is not heavy as well.

953 On the move
If you are buying a tripod for photography on location, be realistic about what you can carry – there is no point buying a high-quality tripod if you leave it at home all the time because it is too much effort to carry.

954 Tube legs
The feature to look for in a small tripod for travelling is strong tubular legs – a tripod like the Gitzo Totalux is ideal for photography on the move.

955 Tripod heads
Consider what sort of tripod head suits your photographic needs. A small ball-and-socket head is fine for 35mm cameras with most lenses. A pan-and-tilt head gives some extra control in handling, and of course when panning. If you want to support a rollfilm camera, or a super-telephoto lens, buy the most robust head you can find. Some pan-and-tilts offer less freedom of movement than ball-and-sockets.

Pan-and-tilt head

956 Heads off
Tripods with removable heads are particularly useful – if you cannot carry the entire tripod with you, you can take off the head and use it independently – resting on a wall, for instance.

957 Boom arm
If you specialize in close-up photography, look for a tripod that takes a boom arm. A boom will allow you to swing the camera right down to your subject at any angle you want.

958 Panoramas
For the photographer who is interested in shooting panoramas, a tripod with a panorama scale marked on the head is ideal. If you already have a tripod, though, you can buy a panorama scale attachment that fits on virtually any tripod.

959 Reversible
If you want to be able to use your tripod for shots from all kinds of angles, buy a tripod with a reversible centre column – it will enable you to use the camera at ground level as well as eye level.

Reversible centre column

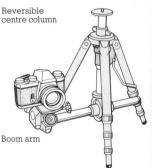

Boom arm

960 Special features

Special features like built-in spirit levels and geared centre columns can be useful – but rigidity should always come first when you make your final choice of tripod.

961 Clamps

Pay close attention to the leg locks when buying your tripod. Look for screw clamps – if abused, quick-release lever clamps on the cheaper models can allow the legs to slip and they may wear.

962 Leg sections

Buy a tripod with as few leg sections as possible. The upper limit is four – and then only if you cannot possibly avoid folding the tripod up to go in a suitcase. Tripods with three leg sections are usually much more stable.

963 Quick release

Quick-release attachments save you having to unscrew the camera every time you want to take a hand-held shot or change the film. They are inexpensive and fit most cameras.

964 Cable release

A cable release is essential if you want to make the most of a tripod's stability. But get one with a lever lock for time exposures.

Lever lock

965 Air release

If you want to fire the shutter from some distance away – for wildlife shots, say – get an air release. This will work with almost any 35mm camera and will allow you to fire the shutter from at least 30ft (10m) from the camera. See Assignment 4.

966 Infra-red release

To fire the camera from the other side of a river, or from up to 65yds (60m) away, you can get a infra-red remote control unit. They avoid the need for trailing cables and are ideal for sports and nature photography.

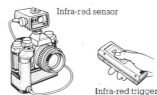

Infra-red sensor

Infra-red trigger

967 Cheap remote control

If you have a motor drive, you can make a cheap remote control system by attaching twin core flex to the contacts on the motor drive – touch the cores together to fire the shutter.

968

Don't try to stand on the leg locks of your tripod, even if you've seen the professionals do it. Only really heavy-duty tripods will stand this type of abuse.

969

Don't use radio-controlled remote shutter releases before you check with the authorities. It could be illegal to use such a device without a licence – even though you may use it with a radio-controlled power boat.

970
Never try to dismantle a flashgun if it is not working properly. Although the batteries look small and harmless enough, the voltages used to power the flash are large, capable of delivering a nasty, even fatal shock.

971
Don't forget that you can fire a flashgun positioned at a distance from the camera by using a slave unit (see **996**).

972
Beware of cheap flashguns if you want to use them for bounced flash. They have to be sufficiently powerful. See **268**.

973 Electronic flash
For utmost versatility, buy the most powerful flashgun you can afford. 'Dedicated' units that automatically synchronize the camera's shutter speed certainly make life easier, but, if you want flash for more than snapshots, it is much better to spend the money on a more powerful independent gun and rely on manual synchronization. If you really want dedicated flash, consider buying a unit with an interchangeable fitting designed to 'dedicate' the gun to your camera.

974 Aperture choice
If you want maximum control over depth of field, look for a flashgun that offers a wide choice of apertures.

975 Recycling
Compare the recycling times of flashguns before you make your choice. If the recycling time is very slow, your subject may lose interest while waiting for the gun to recharge.

976 Swivel head
One of the most important features to look for in a small flashgun is head movement. If the flash head swivels and tilts, you will be able to bounce the light off walls and ceilings.

977 Remote sensor
To take flash pictures with the flash unit some distance from the camera, you need a unit, such as the Vivitar 283, with a detachable light sensor. This is linked to the flash unit with a remote sensor cord, so the sensor can still remain on the camera in order to compute exposure correctly. See **989**.

978 Flash bracket
Most modern flash units are made to fit into the hot shoe of a 35mm camera, but you can achieve better results by mounting the flash on a bracket to one side of the camera. So if you are buying a small flashgun, look for one that can be used in this way.

979 Cover check
For best results, the flash unit must throw light right into the corners of the frame. So before buying a flashgun, check it as follows: fit the unit into the hot shoe and direct the camera at a white wall; photograph the wall using all your lenses. Process the film. The frame should show even overall density of illumination. If the corners are dark, the flash does not cover the picture area well enough. See also **282**.

980 Fish fryer
An ideal light source for studio still lifes, giving even lighting for large subjects, is the 'fish fryer' – multiple flashes mounted behind an opaque screen. Make your own by stretching tracing paper (or Kodatrace) over a frame 18 × 24in (45 × 60cm) and mount two electronic units at 45° above or behind it.

981 Shoe horn

If your camera has no electrical connection in its accessory shoe, you can buy an adaptor that plugs into the sync socket and slides into the camera's accessory shoe. On top of the adaptor is a proper 'hot shoe'.

982 Shoe guns

If you want to buy a large flashgun that works only from a sync socket but your camera has a hot shoe rather than a sync socket, buy an adaptor which slides into the hot shoe and converts it to a sync socket.

983 Battery power

If you expect to use your flashgun heavily, it is well worth getting rechargeable nickel cadmium (NiCad) batteries. Buying new batteries frequently could work out expensive. You can buy flashguns that work from lead acid batteries – like car batteries – but these are heavy items suited only to the professional.

984 Flash power

If you need a really powerful flash system for outdoor shots, you can buy special units that run off a car battery. But a high-power hand gun like the Braun 910 is far more versatile.

985 Twin tube

For portraits with bounced flash, a twin-tube flashgun is ideal. Twin-tube guns have one main head which can be used to bounce light off a ceiling or wall and a smaller secondary head to throw a little light into the eye sockets.

986 Light eyes

If you can't afford a twin-tube flash (985), you can achieve almost the same effect very cheaply by taping a white plastic spoon to the back of the flash reflector. This will throw light into the subject's eye sockets when you are bouncing flash in exactly the same way as a twin-tube would.

987 On reflection

A folding reflector, fitting easily into the camera bag, is one of the most useful pieces of lighting equipment – see 277. If you take many portraits, buy a gold one as well, to give skin tones a warm, golden glow. See also 988.

988 Portable diffuser

For soft light wherever you want it, particularly for portraits, nature and still life shots, buy a folding diffuser ring.

989 Umbrellas

For softer lighting in the studio, buy an inexpensive stand and reflective umbrella. But to use these effectively, you must have a powerful flash gun with a swivel head and a remote sensor (977) – otherwise the sensor will expose for the umbrella, not the subject.

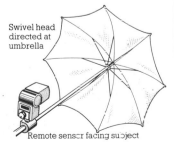

Swivel head directed at umbrella

Remote sensor facing subject

990
Don't bother with flash meter if you only work with a single portable flash – meters are only really essential for multiple flash or when you can vary the power of your flashgun.

991
Don't forget that flash can destroy the atmosphere of a shot. If the available light from domestic lamps is insufficient, you can replace the normal bulbs with photoflood bulbs. These give out much more light, but never leave them switched on for more than a few seconds because they heat up quickly and may burn the lamp shades. Set up the shot with normal bulbs and only insert the photofloods when ready to shoot. See also **998, 999**.

992
Avoid a flashgun that switches itself off after a few minutes if you use your flash frequently. This facility may save battery power, but can be a real nuisance if you miss shots because of waiting for the gun to get ready again.

993
Don't buy studio lighting equipment unless you are sure you will take full advantage of it – it is remarkable what you can achieve with a couple of portable flashguns and a little improvisation. See also **994**.

994
Don't use multiple studio lighting equipment in your home without checking the electrical supply can take the load. Consult an electrician.

995 Zoom flash
If you want to use flash with a wide variety of lenses, it may be worth buying one of the expensive zoom flashes which alter the width of the beam to suit the lens in use. If you do buy a flash with a zoom head, look carefully at the calculator dial. Since the telephoto setting concentrates the light on a smaller area, you should theoretically have more power at your dsposal and this means that you can use either smaller apertures or shoot subjects further away at any given aperture. But some of the less sophisticated zoom guns do not allow you to exploit these benefits to the full.

996 Multiple flash
For out-of-the-ordinary lighting you need to use more than one flashgun – but multiple flashguns must still be fired from a single socket. The cheapest solution is to use an adaptor that splits the flash sync cable into three ways. But by far the best method, since it avoids long lengths of trailing wires, is a slave unit that triggers off a flashgun instantly it 'sees' the flash from another gun fired conventionally.

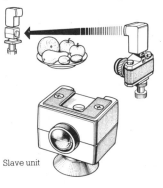

Slave unit

997 Hiring lights
Unless you expect to recoup the expense of large studio lighting units by selling pictures, hire them only for special sessions.

998 Low-cost lights
If you want the wide range of effects that only multiple lighting can give, but cannot afford a complete set of flashguns and slave units, consider buying an inexpensive tungsten system.

999 Long-life tungsten
One of the problems with tungsten light is that bulbs get extremely hot during a long session. Another is their limited life. To keep lamps cooler and prolong their life, fit a dimmer switch as a main control and only use full power when metering and shooting.

1000 Improvised spot
A slide projector makes an excellent spotlight for small close-up subjects. Just cut a hole with 1in (2.5cm) diameter in a slide mount. Insert this in the holder and focus the beam.

1001 Colour temperature
If you do plenty of work in mixed lighting, consider buying a colour temperature meter to help achieve a high standard of colour correction. Buy the most versatile model possible. Some only measure red-blue light. If you shoot in fluorescent light, you need one that measures red-green light as well, and gives two types of reading: one for light balancing with, for instance, Wratten filters, and one for Colour Correction filters.

DARKROOM EQUIPMENT

1002 Darkroom kits
Many manufacturers sell complete darkroom kits, and these are generally value for money if you are starting out on home processing. Watch for kits that include unnecessary extras; detect such extras by comparing the contents of different kits and asking the dealer about the function of suspect items.

1003 Developing tanks
These are made in plastic or stainless steel. Stainless steel has the advantage over plastic of allowing loading even when the spiral is wet. It requires a different loading technique to the plastic tank, which many find easier, and a few more awkward. Before buying, it is worth exploring each type by going to a dealer who will let you experiment with a roll of waste film.

1004 Daylight tanks
Special daylight' tanks are available which allow film to be loaded without a darkroom.

1005 Film washer
You can wash film in an open tank under water, but a purpose-made film washer will do the job more quickly and efficiently. Some will wash films in just five minutes.

1006 Film wipers
When buying a pair of wipers, look for lightweight, flimsy blades – they work well and are less likely to scratch film than heavy blades.

1007 Measuring cylinders
For accurate measuring, you need a range of cylinders – say 3½ fl.oz (100ml), 9 fl.oz (250ml) and 18 fl.oz (500ml). The small cylinder is particularly important if you use concentrated developers.

1008 Other measures
At a pinch, you can improvise measuring cylinders for chemicals used in black and white developing and printing. This is because dilutions are all by proportion, not by specific volume. For example, 1 – 9 could mean one egg cup, or one whisky glass, of developer to nine of water.

1009 Thermometers
Mercury thermometers are highly accurate, more so than spirit thermometers, but they are expensive and fragile. For b/w developing and printing, buy a mercury and a spirit thermometer. Check the accuracy of the second against the first, store the mercury thermometer safely, and use the spirit one for routine work. For colour work, see 1207.

1010
Don't leave containers used for mixing chemicals where they might be used inadvertently for food or drink. This is obviously most important if you improvise (see 1008) with kitchen measuring jugs. Paint a warning on such items and store them securely.

1011
Don't leave chemicals in unlabelled containers, and if there are children in the house, keep containers in a lockable cupboard.

DARKROOM EQUIPMENT

1012
Don't buy a condenser enlarger for black and white work if you do much retouching on negatives. The high-contrast image produced by this type of enlarger makes retouching marks show up.

1013
Don't put too much faith in improvised print processing trays such as garden seed trays – they may not be rigid enough for easy agitation and they can take up chemicals.

1014
Don't forget to examine the negative carrier in an enlarger you are interested in buying. Ideally it should take both glassless and glass negative carriers. The first is for general work, and eliminates the formation of Newton's rings – multi-coloured marks which may occur when two sheets of glass are pressed together. The second is for critical work when the negative has to be absolutely flat.

1015 Enlargers
Most enlargers for colour work use a diffuse light source, but if you only shoot in black and white, consider buying a condenser enlarger which gives a high-contrast image suitable for giant enlargements.

1016 Colour drawers
If you only want to make colour prints occasionally, an enlarger with a filter drawer is probably adequate. Making colour prints by fitting individual filters is more laborious than with a colour mixing head – see 1017 – but the extra expense is rarely justified for an amateur.

1017 Colour head
A colour head, which allows you to dial in the required filtration for colour printing instantly without tedious manual filter changing, is worth the expense if colour printing is a major leisure activity. See also 1016.

1018 Format
Before you decide on an enlarger, make sure you will be happy with the format (see 47): many cheaper enlargers only accept 35mm negatives.

1019 Smooth and sturdy
Look for an enlarger with a sturdy column, and check that the enlarger head moves smoothly up and down.

1020 Giant prints
If you want to make giant prints, get an enlarger with a head that can be tilted horizontally so that the image can be projected on to a wall.

1021 Quality lens
Buy a quality lens such as a Schneider or Nikon even if it costs as much as the enlarger itself. It will give your prints real edge and quality, and you will still be able to use it if you ever upgrade your enlarger.

1022 Marking time
An enlarger timer will leave your hands free for burning-in and dodging (1186, 1184) and ensures consistent exposure times.

1023 Beat it
A cheap alternative to a timer is a metronome – it enables you to time print exposures by ear so that you can look at the print for dodging and burning-in. In an emergency, any regular rhythm – even a dripping tap – will do for longer exposures.

1024
Some find a foot switch for the enlarger is all but essential because it leaves the hands free to manipulate the print. See 1111.

1025 Colour drum
The easiest way to process colour prints is in a special drum. If you can afford it, buy a drum with a motorized base – it makes the job far easier and ensures consistent results.

1026 Special printers
If you have nowhere that you can set up as a darkroom, you can buy a special enlarger that can be used on the living room table – the only problem is that the range of print sizes is limited.

PROCESSING AND DARKROOM

Best results, commercially and at home

1027

Don't automatically assume it is the processing firm's or lab's fault when you receive prints or negatives with some serious failing such as consistent over- or underexposure, or damage such as scratches. In both cases, and in many others, it is sadly much easier for the lab to say it is your fault, or your equipment's, than for you to prove otherwise. However, don't be afraid to complain if you really suspect the processor is to blame. Arm yourself with a second opinion from a friendly professional or photo dealer, and with this back-up, approach the lab. Poor-quality prints should be done again free of charge. For damaged negatives there is often no adequate compensation. If the work is unique or valuable, see **1065**.

1028

Don't expect machine-made prints to show the whole negative area. Slight cropping on all sides is unavoidable. See also **209**.

1029 Remember

Processing laboratories make standard-sized (i.e. postcard-sized) amateur prints on automatic machines unless hand printing is especially requested. The machines make acceptable, often excellent prints of most subjects if well managed; however, they do not give their best results with pictures where one colour is dominant. In this case, hand printing (**1033**) is the solution.

1030

Processing laboratories are divided broadly into those with a mainly amateur clientele, and those who serve mainly professionals. The chief exception is Kodak's Kodachrome transparency service, which Kodak alone is qualified to operate, except in the US.

1031

As an amateur, shop around for the best developing and printing service in your area. Some fast services produce appalling results – flat, muddy, unreal colours. Examine results friends have had from different firms. Don't go by the sample prints displayed in retailers as evidence of a lab's work. If in doubt, have developing and printing done through a reputable camera dealer, who is most likely to use a sound lab. See also **59, 72** and **1027**.

1032 Standards

One difference between the amateur and professional lab (see **1030**) is that amateur firms tend to use the same developer for all black and white films. The professional firms use appropriately matched developers, so giving better results for the discerning.

1033 Hand printing

Most amateur labs offer a hand printing service. This means that the prints are made individually in an enlarger, rather than on an automatic machine. The service costs more, but it enables you to specify the size of your print, how it is to be cropped (but see **1034**) and some special controls, i.e. dodging and burning in (**1184–1188**).

1034 Auto-selective

Some labs offer selective enlargement of part of the image when they make machine prints. This costs less than a cropped hand print, but you will not be able to specify the cropping so precisely.

1035 Crop instructions

If you want a cropped image, the easiest way to show a lab exactly what you want is to mark up an existing print with a Chinagraph (grease pencil). The marks rub off easily with a clean tissue.

1036 Abroad
Labs in underdeveloped countries may give variable, or downright poor, quality. If you have to get film processed in a doubtful lab, consider running off a test roll and having this processed first.

1037 Precautions
Replace exposed film in the manufacturer's plastic container – especially if it has to be posted. Apart from the obvious danger of physical damage, there is always the chance of damp.

1038
When you run off the first few frames of a newly loaded film, photograph your name written out in block capitals. If the film gets mislaid at a lab, it can be easily identified this way.

1039
There is always the chance a lab may not follow processing instructions. The only precautions are finding a reliable lab and making instructions totally clear, and brief. See **1040**.

1040
Space is provided on cassettes and rollfilm for briefest processing instructions, i.e. '400 ISO exposed at 800 ISO; push one stop'. If the same instruction applies to several films, write it on a slip of paper and fasten films and instruction together with an elastic band.

1041
If you send a batch of film for processing, each roll with different processing instructions,
you can make doubly sure there is no confusion by photographing your hand on each roll. Roll one shows the hand with a single finger raised: roll two with two fingers, and so on. A single sheet of instructions can then refer to the films by number.

1042 Mixed batches
If you have a mixed lot of film for processing, some requiring special processing, some not, it helps the lab if you sort them into batches with instructions clearly supplied – see **1040**.

1043 Bulk loading
If you load your film from bulk (see **88**) put exactly 36 frames in cassettes to be sent for lab processing. Some labs use spirals for processing and to fit the film on to the spiral may mean cutting off frames. See also **1045**.

1044
It is vital to mark the film type on a cassette containing bulk-loaded film (**88**) if having it processed commercially.

1045 Clip damage
If you have squeezed an extra frame or even two on to the end of a roll of film to be processed commercially, you may find these are damaged by the clips which labs have to use to hold films. See also **1043**.

1046
Beware of 'free film' and processing offers – see **59**; see also **826**.

1047
Don't swap processors just for the sake of it. If you find a firm satisfactory, stay with them. You can judge your results more critically if processing is consistent. See **157**.

1048
Check that a lab can give different print surface finishes before committing your film.

1049
Don't forget to leave your name and phone number if dealing direct with a processing lab.

1050
Beware of labs offering a wide range of services. This is convenient, but the quality may not be consistently high. Labs which offer just one service usually give fast results and consistent quality.

1051
Don't expect a new colour print to match one the lab did last time. Colour balance is to some extent a matter of taste. Send the old print with your order, and ask the lab to match it.

DEALING WITH PROCESSING FIRMS

1052
Avoid having contact prints made. It is usually an expensive service, likely to cost more than having a complete set of machine prints of the whole film. From these it is easy to select photos for reprinting or enlarging, and it is easier to mark up an image (see **1035**) this size for selective enlargement than it is a tiny contact

1053 Prints from slides
There are several different ways of making prints from slides; the most usual, and cheapest, result is called an R type. (Prints from colour negatives are called C types.)

1054
If you want a particularly high-quality print from a slide, or one that is slower to fade than an R type (**1053**) when subjected to bright sunlight for long periods, find a lab that makes 'Cibachrome' prints. They are good value.

1055
The E6 process – used for Ektachrome and similar films – can be manipulated to alter the colour balance of slides. If you need this facility, check to see what labs offer it. Expect an extra charge.

1056 Cost cutting
It is usually much cheaper to have machine prints made at the same time as the film is processed. If you want to examine the negatives in order to decide on which to have printed, check first how much will be charged for the prints made as a separate order.

1057
If you require a large number of identical prints from a single negative, shop around for the best deal. Discounts ought to be offered for long runs.

1058 Slack season
If you have plenty of colour printing to be done and it is not urgent, wait until the slack season. This runs through late autumn (fall), winter and early spring, when labs have unused capacity and may well offer a special deal on large orders from regular customers.

1059 Special services
A few labs offer mini prints, measuring about $3\frac{1}{2} \times 2\frac{1}{2}$ in (9×6cm) with double-sided sticky tape on the backs as an optional extra. You have to order at least 100, but the prints are relatively cheap and are useful for attaching to a pre-printed greetings or business card. For an extra charge many labs will add lettering to a margin left on the print; these too can be useful for business cards or identification purposes at conferences or other large functions.

1060
Labs that specialize in processing wedding photographs usually offer a standard montaging service. Photos can be montaged on to existing images of wineglasses, candles, flowers or even hearts if that is what seems appropriate.

1061
Some labs will create in-dividual montages of your own specification. You will have to prepare a rough freehand sketch for them to work to; better, take photocopies of the prints to be combined in the montage, cut them out and stick them to paper, assembled in the way you wish.

1062
When you want a print mounted or laminated, preferably use the same lab for the whole job. If you use two, they will probably blame each other for mistakes.

1063 Wrong light source
If you find your colour prints have a strange colour cast overall, or in parts, it may be because you shot the film in unsuitable artificial lighting – see **67.** Hand printing could remove the cast, or improve it. The same applies to colour prints made from slides, but not to slides themselves – see **66** for full details

1064 Chromogenic film
This type of black and white film – see **84** – should be processed on its own for best results. Some labs put it in with other film to cut costs. Check your lab's method.

1065 Liability
Most laboratories claim that their liability in the event of loss or damage to film while in their possession is limited to the cost of replacement unexposed film. The legal force of this is doubtful, and varies in different countries. However, proving a lab is in the wrong is likely to be difficult – see **1027** – so if work has a market value, play safe by insuring it.

1066 Rapport
It is worth getting to know the printer who handles your work if you place plenty of it with one lab. If you want prints for specific purposes, inform the printer; he will know, for instance, the requirements for newspaper and magazine reproduction. If you need an exhibition print, meet and discuss your exact needs. Respect any advice that is offered until it is proved false or unhelpful – a tension-free relationship is essential.

1067
Don't be vague or constantly change your mind about printing requirements if a lab is doing a special job for you. This is irritating for the printer. Respect the professional's experience and advice; remember the most beautiful pictures you have taken only exist as a roll of celluloid until processed and printed.

SETTING UP A DARKROOM

1068
Don't store or use electrical equipment near the taps (faucets).

1069
Don't lead cables across the floor – they can be a hazard in the dark.

1070
Never install conventional light switches in a darkroom. The main white light, inspection light and safelight should be controlled by cord pull switches as in a bathroom.

1071
Watch for loose floorboards in a darkroom. If you tread on one during exposure of paper under the enlarger, the enlarger could move, causing 'unsharpness' in the print. See also 1073, 1074–1075.

1072
Test a darkroom's lightproofing by sitting in it with the lights out for at least five minutes. Your eyes, accustomed to the dark, will pick up any stray light. Total black-out is vital for colour work, not so critical for black and white.

1073 Always
Choose a room for the darkroom where the floor is firm, preferably solid. This minimizes vibration which can be transmitted via the enlarger on its bench, taking the edge off image sharpness. Heavy lorries, and railways passing close by can also cause vibration.

1074
Attach the enlarger bench to a solid wall and see 1073.

1075 Below stairs
Basements are usually the best locations for darkrooms. They are certainly better than attics, where the temperature is less stable – hot in summer and cold in winter.

1076 Workbench height
About 36in (90cm) is the right height for darkroom worktops.

1077 Surfacing a bench
Apply an easily cleaned white plastic laminate to give maximum reflection, and so better vision when the safelight is switched on.

1078 On the walls
Paint the darkroom the same colour as the safelight. Any stray light (for example from the enlarger lamp housing) will be reflected off the walls as 'safe'. And the darkroom will be brighter to work in.

1079 Wider horizons
To give a feeling of openness to a darkroom and minimize claustrophobia, cut a window

to an adjoining room and cover it with a sheet of red Perspex (Plexiglas). To test its safety, see 1085. Fit a blind to the window for black-out when this is necessary.

1080 Lightproofing
For windows, probably the most convenient method of lightproofing is an opaque blind or drape with the edges running in a specially made frame.

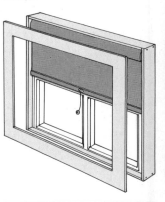

1081
A cheaper alternative to 1080 is wooden sheeting, cut about 2in (5cm) larger all round than the window. Stick foam round the edges and attach.

1082
To make doors lightproof, buy foam draught proofing strips and coat them with black paint. Along the bottom of the door pin a strip of carpet.

1083 The safelight
There is really only one position for the safelight – over the developing tray. Elsewhere

it will probably cast your shadow over the print as you watch it develop. (See **1092** for an explanation of safelights.)

1084 Inspection lamp
Locate it over the fixer tray for best viewing of finished prints under white light.

1085 Makeshift safelamp
A bicycle's rear lamp can make a useful makeshift safelamp for b/w print processing. Test it first by exposing a strip of film to the lamp, keeping one section inside the cassette or lightproof container. The lamp is only safe if both sections are clear after development.

1086 Drying rack
An old-fashioned plate rack, with wooden pegs, is ideal for drying darkroom equipment. Just hang items on the pegs. Position rack above the sink

1087 Positioning towels
A towel is essential in a darkroom; if possible hang it between the wet and dry areas (see **1091**) so the hands can be dried each time you pass.

1088 Exit lobby
In a permanent darkroom, some means of leaving the room without letting in white light can be convenient. Build a partition around the door from floor to ceiling to create a lobby and curtain it off with heavy black material. Anyone leaving the room goes into the lobby, draws the curtain, opens the door and leaves without fogging printing papers in use.

1089 Dust problem
If your darkroom is exceptionally dusty, examine the bottom edges of the skirting boards (baseboards). An appreciable gap between them and the floor could act as a dust trap. Prevent it from doing so by sealing the gap with a hard-setting mastic

1090 Shelving
Install open shelving rather than cupboards. Cupboard doors get in the way when open – and can cause bruised shins when only dimly visible under the safelight. Have separate shelves for printing paper and chemicals. Locate shelves for paper below the workbench; stretching over the bench up to a height for heavy boxes is not convenient. (Stack boxes with the contrast grade label visible.) Locate shelves for chemicals under the sink; above the workbench level there is always the chance they will be knocked down on top of some valuable piece of work.

1091 'Dry' and 'wet'
Establish a 'dry' and 'wet' area in your darkroom: organize the space so they are well separated. The dry area must feature all equipment required for operating the enlarger – shelves for paper, dodges, timer, and of course the enlarger itself. Nothing even remotely wet should ever reach this area. Printing papers can be ruined even by the lightest touch of a finger dampened with developer. Even cups of coffee should be banned: a damp spot on the workbench could be where you put down negatives.

1092
Don't use more powerful bulbs than recommended in safelights. They will overheat, and perhaps impair the 'safety' of the lamp. (Safelights – essential darkroom equipment – enable you to handle photographic paper in the dim light they give cut because photographic papers are insensitive to certain shades of red and green-yellow light. Check safelamp requirements from the instruction sheet supplied with photographic paper. It will specify the ideal shade of safelamp, size of bulb and height for hanging above the developer tray.)

1093
Don't surface a darkroom floor with any material that is not washable. Lino tiles are ideal.

1094
Never let a darkroom get dirty. Dust gets into the enlarger housing with surprising ease; once there it can cause specks on finished prints. Keep dust down by washing or at least mopping the floor regularly. Wipe worktops with a damp cloth. Dust shelves. See **1089**.

1095
Never leave trays unwashed after a darkroom session. Once in a while, clean the developer tray (print developer leaves heavy deposits) with a solution of ferrocyanide and print fixer.

1096
Don't use a mercury thermometer for run-of-the-mill b/w darkroom work – see **1009**. However, it is worth using one for critical work because it responds so quickly.

1097
Check the spare thermometer, if you have one, against the master one (**1207**). There is often a significant variation between thermometers.

1098
Don't use thermometers with red spirit in them. It is almost impossible to read under a safelight.

1099
Don't store thermometers on shelves: they have a habit of rolling off and breaking. Store them upright in a jar.

1100 Darkroom habits
Maintain a high degree of organization on the 'dry' area of a darkroom (**1091**). Develop the habit of returning everything used in connection with the enlarger to an appointed place. See **1101** to **1104**.

1101
A sheet of wood drilled with holes, fitted with pegs, and hung an inch or so forward from the wall makes a useful storage centre for tape, scissors and other items.

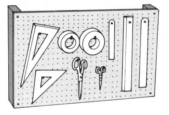

1102
A magnetic strip, of the type sold for holding kitchen knives, can be handy for holding metal objects in place.

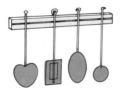

1103
A pinboard (cork tiles are a convenient material) on the wall near the enlarger is useful for pinning up notes.

1104
A household torch is useful for finding things in dark corners.

1105 The wet area
This features all the trays and chemicals for processing, plus the sink. Running water is highly convenient, but not essential in a darkroom. You can improvise with buckets of water. Mixing chemicals is in any case best done outside a darkroom: the slightest splash can contaminate papers.

1106
Walls surrounding the sink should be washable.

1107
Sinks with flat draining boards are useful for eliminating excess water from prints.

1108
If water pressure is low in your darkroom, so that waterflow is insufficient for thorough washing of prints (see **1294**), try replacing the pipes with ones of a larger bore.

1109 Drains
Check with manufacturers that materials in your drainage system are suitable for chemicals that you will be using. The plastic compounds used in most drainage systems can withstand most uses, but extremely hot water, and some acids, could damage them.

1110
Regularly flush the drain serving your darkroom with a solution of caustic soda.

1111 Electrical
Wire a footswitch into the enlarger circuit so you can

switch the enlarger on and off without using your hands. This is extremely useful when dodging and burning in (see 1184–1188).

1112 In the dark
Small luminous pads can be bought for sticking on to switches and handles – useful if you have trouble locating them in dim safelighting.

1113 Safety
A high degree of electrical safety can be achieved in a permanent darkroom by having an electrician fit an earth leakage circuit breaker.

1114 Safe for white light?
If your white light switch (but see 1070) is next to the safelight switch it is a good idea to fit a card or hardboard flap over the white light switch so you have to lift it before turning the white light on. With this 'reminder' you are unlikely to absent-mindedly switch on the white light while printing papers are out on the bench, in the developer or only just placed in the fixing bath, still likely to fog.

1115 Extended switch
If the darkroom white light is operated (as it should be – see 1070) by a pull switch, you can rig up an extremely useful extension running right round the darkroom. Simply run the cord through an eyelet and attach an extension cord of a suitable length. Run this through further eyelets about 6in (15cm) above head height. Use it for switching the white light on and off wherever you happen to be standing.

1116 Oversize baseboard
An extra-large enlarger baseboard, which protrudes over the edge of the workbench, allows a more comfortable standing or sitting position when working the enlarger. It is tiring to have to reach forward for any length of time.

1117 Trays
Use large trays for chemicals. Trays the same size as printing paper make the paper difficult to handle.

1118 Ventilation
Adequate ventilation is vital. Make vents in doors or windows. Fit simple flaps as light traps. The vent size should be no less than 9 × 9in (22 × 22cm) for a room 10 × 10ft (3 × 3m).

1119 Telephone
A darkroom extension saves time, and wasted paper.

1120
Don't expose prints with an enlarger that rocks on the workbench. If it is proving difficult to make the enlarger stable, fix the head of the column to a wall behind.

1121
Don't use paper towels in a darkroom: they make dust when you tear them off the roll.

1122
Avoid siting print drying apparatus, or simply drying prints, in the darkroom. Ideally, this process is done in an adjacent area or room. The heat and moisture created make for uncomfortable working conditions, and can upset controlled temperatures needed for development.

1123
Don't forget to shake all the dust out if you are using a changing bag to load the film.

1124
Beware of dampness on the spiral; it can make the film stick. Dry the spiral in warm air beforehand – not direct heat, which may warp it. And wash the spiral thoroughly after use – chemical deposits can build up quickly.

1125
Never force a film into a spiral even when it seems stuck – you may tear it. If you find yourself getting frustrated, put the film or film and spiral in the tank – provided it is clean and dry – put the lid on, then switch on the light and take a breather.

1126 Preparation
The key to success with b/w film processing is careful preparation. Make sure everything you need falls easily to hand and all equipment is clean and dry. Read manufacturer's instructions.

1127 Filter clean
Mixing beakers and thermometers must be cleaned thoroughly before use – and the best way is with filtered water. You can buy purpose-made filters that take a narrow-gauge hose to give you a brisk jet of water ideal for force washing. Even if your water seems pure and particle-free, it is worth using a filter to be on the safe side.

1128 Loading the tank
All films must be loaded into the developing tank in complete darkness, but if you haven't got a darkroom, a purpose-made zip-up changing bag will do.

1129 Practice run
Before you attempt to load an exposed film into the spiral try a few dummy runs with old film. Try first in the light so that you can see what goes on, then move into the darkroom.

1130 Emulsion side
Always load the emulsion side of the film inwards – the emulsion side naturally curls inwards and this assists loading.

1131 Can opener
The simplest way to open film cassettes is with a bottle opener – as a last resort, you can thump the protruding end of the spool hard on the bench, but this can cause damage.

1132 Cutting corners
When you're loading film into a plastic spiral, cut off the corners to give a smoother load – it is the sharp corners of the film end which tend to snag.

1133 Sticking spiral
If the film sticks in the spiral, try wiggling the film sideways. If this doesn't work, unload a few inches and start again, wiggling the film at the same time if necessary.

1134 Stainless steel
Use a stainless-steel spiral if you have difficulty with films sticking in plastic spirals. They are only a little more expensive; but see **1003**.

1135 Heavy metal
If you do plenty of film processing, use a heavy-gauge stainless-steel spiral. This may be more expensive, but it will last longer than a cheaper model and is less likely to lose shape and become difficult to load.

1136 Multi-roll tanks

When processing a single film in a multi-roll tank, include the empty spirals in the tank to prevent the full spiral sliding up and down.

1137

When processing more than one roll of film in a multi-roll tank, load the spirals in alternate directions to give better agitation.

1138 Pre-warming

Once you have loaded the tank, put it in a water bath at the processing temperature to warm it up ready for the developer.

1139 Warming developer

The best way to get the developer to the right temperature is to mix it cool and then stand the beaker in a bowl of warm water to heat it to the correct temperature – this is much easier than mixing it warm and cooling it under a running tap (faucet).

1140

Developer has to be at 68°F (20°C) for best results, so check the temperature immediately before pouring it into the tank.

1141 Pouring developer

Use a funnel and pour the developer into the tank as fast as possible to ensure even development. Hold the tank at an angle of 45° to increase the pouring rate. Overfill the tank to ensure that the film is completely immersed – even if only one roll is being loaded.

1142 Bubbles

Start timing immediately the tank is filled, but tap the tank sharply several times to dislodge trapped air bubbles which may otherwise cause undeveloped spots on the film surface.

1143 Agitation

Proper agitation is essential – too much or too little can mean the film is wrongly developed. Standardize your procedure and stick to it. A typical agitation routine might be to invert the tank once or twice every half-minute – this is usually more efficient than a twiddle-stick.

1144 Temperature

Correct development temperature is important – so keep the tank in a bath of warm water at 68°F (20°C) for the entire process. See also 1151.

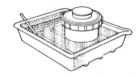

1145 Washing

Wash the film in running water for no more than a minute, filling and emptying the tank three times.

1146 Stop bath

A stop bath stops development instantly and, by preventing carry-over of developer, prolongs the life of the fixer. You can buy stop baths ready-made or mix your own with a 3% solution of glacial acetic acid in a well-ventilated room.

1147

Never be tempted to stir chemicals with the thermometer – it is very fragile.

1148

Don't leave chemicals in half-filled bottles. If you cannot find a bottle of the right size, fill the bottle with marbles to raise the level until all air is excluded – or better still, buy a collapsible container that can be squeezed to force the air out.

1149

Never use discoloured developer – fresh developer is always colourless.

1150

Be careful not to wash the film for too long after development if you are using plain water – development continues until the film is in the fixer unless you use an acid stop bath. A minute is quite long enough for the interim wash.

1151

Avoid sudden drops in temperature – such as plunging the film into a cold wash. The shock will cause 'crazy paving' cracks on the film, technically known as reticulation.

1152
Never use exhausted fixer – if the film looks cloudy after the normal fixing time (see tip 1158), the fixer is exhausted and should be thrown away before you process the next roll of film.

1153
Don't use washing-up liquid as a wetting agent. It is little cheaper than the real thing, but it does not do the job properly: and it sometimes contains additives that can leave smears on the film surface.

1154
Don't leave the film lying around after the final rinse or it will dry streakily.

1155
Never smoke near drying film – the ash can be very harmful to the emulsion.

1156
Don't leave the film out to gather dust after drying – cut it into strips and file away in purpose-made paper sleeves.

1157 Fixing
Remember to agitate the fixer vigorously for the first half-minute, then invert the tank every ten seconds for the entire fixing period.

1158 Milky film
If the film seems slightly milky after the recommended fixing time, put the spiral back in the tank and fix for a little longer. See 1152.

1159 Washing
The best way to wash film is under running water – either direct a hose into the tank or remove the lid and place the tank under a tap (faucet) for 20 to 30 minutes. See also 1160.

1160
If you cannot use running water (see 1159) fill and empty the tank at least once every two minutes, and shake the tank vigorously for 20 minutes.

1161
If the water is cold – say at 50°F (10°C) – increase washing time by 50%.

1162 Wetting agent
Use wetting agent in the final rinse to ensure even drying of film. You need such small amounts of wetting agent that you will find it easiest, and most economical, to dilute the whole bottle of wetting agent with nine parts of water (this is the usual dilution recommended in the instructions). If you then mix 1 fluid oz of this stock solution with a pint of water (alternatively 10ml with 200ml) you should get the right dilution.

1163 Clipped
Attach a film clip to the 'free' end of the film before you withdraw it from the spiral and use this to handle the film – wet film is very easily damaged.

1164 Hanging
Hang the film to dry in a dust-free environment – preferably a proper drying cupboard. Settle dust before hanging by spraying the area with water from a plant spray.

1165 Clothes peg
To stop film from curling up, you need to attach a weight to the end – wooden clothes pegs will do; metal clips are ideal.

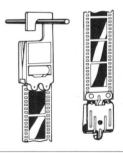

1166 Squeegee
To avoid drying marks, remove excess water from the film immediately you hang it up. A soft rubber squeegee is the ideal method, but make sure there are no tiny grit particles on the blades to scratch the film.

1167 Rapid processing
If you want to process several films quickly, use a high-speed developer – but you must time the development accurately and agitate thoroughly.

1168 Contact prints

A set of contact prints of every black and white film you take is invaluable for reference if stored in a file (1323–1325). A purpose-made contact printing frame organizes a 36-exposure 35mm film so that it fits on to a sheet of 10 × 8 in (25 × 20cm) printing paper. See 1169–1171.

1169 Glass and sponge

If you rarely make contacts and don't want to buy a contact printing frame (1168), tape negatives to the underside of a sheet of glass and rest this on the printing paper. As a base for the whole assembly, a layer of sponge is ideal. See 1170–1171.

1170 Light source

The most convenient light source for making contact prints is the enlarger.

1171 Exposing contacts

To establish the exposure for a contact print (1168), make a test strip (1179–1181) from a strip of negatives taken with the lens cap on the camera. The shortest time that gives a pure black print is the correct exposure time. Set the enlarger at the same height and aperture and you can use this exposure for all your contacts.

1172 Emulsion side down

When loading the negative into the enlarger, remember to place the emulsion side underneath. The emulsion side is matt and less smooth than the non-emulsion side.

1173 Glassless carrier

When using a glassless negative carrier to avoid Newton's rings (see 1014), leave the negative in the enlarger with the lamp switched on for half a minute. This allows any movement due to heat to pass before focusing.

1174 Focusing

For accurate focusing, you need as much light from the enlarger as possible, so open up the lens aperture as wide as possible. Then stop it down for the actual exposure.

1175 Focusing aid

For accurate and easy focusing, use a magnifying focuser: it enables you to examine the actual grain of the negative.

1176 Clamp the negative

Check that the clamps on the enlarger's negative carrier hold all four edges of the negative down firmly – any gap means that the edge of the negative will be out of focus.

1177 On the level

For sharp prints, the enlarger's negative carrier and baseboard must be perfectly parallel. Use a spirit level to check, or measure opposite sides of the image on the baseboard – they must be equal in length.

1178
Beware of dust – it is the bane of every printer. No amount of the control over exposure and processing can compensate for a print covered in white spots, which are the shadows of dust specks. The worst place for dust is on the negative – of course any dust on the negative will be enlarged just like the negative. So it is important to clean the negative carrier and the negative thoroughly before printing. The best cleaning method is a powerful blow brush. Quite often, you will find that you cannot remove dust specks from the negative because they have stuck to the film while it was drying. If so, you may be able to remove them by washing the film once more and hanging it to dry in a dust-free environment. Ultimately, though, the solution is to keep dust in the darkroom down as much as possible. See also 1089, 1094, 1106, 1121, 1123, 1155, 1156, 1164.

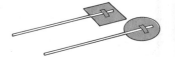

1179
Don't leave chemicals standing in open dishes overnight – they will be useless next day.

1180
Don't write off unsharp prints to negative faults – the problem could well be your enlarging. Prints which lack definition due to inaccurate focusing of the enlarger usually look rather gloomy and grey, with the shadows spreading into the highlights. An unsharp negative gives the opposite effect.

1181
Don't try to dodge in (1187) too large an area – it will probably show up horribly.

1182 Test strips
To find out the correct exposure for each print, make a test strip on a small strip of paper cut from a large sheet under safelighting. To make a test strip, place this small strip on the enlarger baseboard and cover it with opaque card. Move the card to uncover a fifth of the strip. Switch on the enlarger – preferably by smoothly swinging the red filter clear – and expose for five seconds. Switch off and move the card to uncover a further fifth of the strip and make another five-second exposure. Continue to uncover the strip in steps until the whole strip has been exposed. This will give you a range of test exposures from 5–25 secs. Then process the strip normally. The alternative to a test strip is an enlarging exposure meter – expensive and not infallible. See also **856.**

1183 Ready-made wedge
For really easy test strips, buy a test 'wedge' with densities graded to match exposure times – so you only make one exposure.

1184 Vertical strips
To ensure that the test strip is representative of the print as a whole, run the strips vertically across to include land and sky.

1185 Low shake
To minimize the possibility of vibration during exposure, hold a piece of opaque card over the paper while you swing the filter out of the light path. Only remove the card to begin the exposure a second or two later when vibration has died down.

1186 Exposure timer
The best way to ensure accurate exposures with minimum of vibration, if you are using a cold cathode enlarger or an enlarger with a glass negative carrier, is to use an exposure timer.

1187 Dodging
If shadows are too dark to show any detail even when most of the print is correctly exposed, you can hold back exposure in these areas by covering them for some of the exposure – a technique known as 'dodging'.

1188 Dodging tool
Dodging covers (see 1187) should be cut from card to the same shape as the shadow area to be dodged. But you can make yourself a 'universal' dodging tool with a circle of card on the end of a piece of wire. The card needs to be moved slightly to and fro during dodging to avoid a hard edge and, more importantly, you must swivel the wire handle over a wide angle to stop its shadow registering on the print.

1189 Burning-in

If the correct exposure is too short for detail to appear in the highlights, 'burn' them in. This means giving the correct exposure to all the print, then covering all but the highlights while you give a little more exposure. See 1190–1191.

1190 Burning-in tools

Most burning-in (1189) can be done with your hands. With a little practice, you will find this the quickest and easiest method. If you have a very complex piece of burning-in to do, cut a card mask to shape, but make sure that the side of the card facing the enlarger baseboard is black or red so that you don't reflect light back on to the print.

1191 Burning big

Always burn-in (1189) an area slightly larger than you need – it shows up less this way.

1192 Into the developer

For even development, raise the dish at one end, slide the paper quickly into the shallow end, then immediately lower the dish so that a wave of developer covers the paper from end to end. During development, rock the dish by lifting different corners.

1193 Standard time

For consistent results, use a standard development time for every print. Then if you want to increase contrast for a particular print, you can extend your standard time slightly. If you want to reduce contrast, shorten your standard time.

1194 Farmer's Reducer

To give extra sparkle to highlights, wipe the print after fixing with a sponge soaked in Farmer's Reducer. Simply wipe quickly across the whole print and immediately wash the print in cold running water. Don't pause to see the effect until the print is in the water. Remove from the water, fix briefly, then wash normally.

1195

To dodge in small shadow areas after the print has fixed, dab the area with Farmer's Reducer on a small brush or cotton bud, then proceed as described in 1194.

1196 Paper grades

Exploit various grades of printing paper to bring the best out of individual negatives. If the negative is lacking in contrast – perhaps because of underexposure – use a high-contrast 'hard' paper (grade 4 or 5) for some sparkle. For a high-contrast negative – perhaps one that is overdeveloped – use a soft grade (0 or 1).

1197 Multi-grade

To save buying complete boxes of grades you might only use rarely, buy multi-grade paper. This gives a range of different grades on a single sheet of paper – you select the grade simply by printing through an appropriate coloured filter.

1198
Be careful when using tongs – they can crease photographic paper. Rubber gloves give you much more feel, especially important when handling very large prints.

1199
Don't use metal tongs to agitate chemicals when dish processing. You can easily scratch the emulsion. Plastic tongs are best.

PROCESSING COLOUR FILM

1200
Don't store fresh colour film processing chemicals at temperatures below 55°F (13°C). Partly used chemicals should be kept above 61°F (16°C).

1201
Don't use your fingers or a squeegee to wipe down the film before drying – if the final stabilizer is correct, colour film will drain dry without any drying marks – unlike b/w film.

1202
Don't wash colour film again after the stabilizing bath – it helps the film to dry properly.

1203 Colour process kits
The simplest way to learn how to process colour film is to buy a basic kit for your favourite film, complete with step-by-step directions. See also tips 1123–1125, 1127–1137.

1204 The right process
Although most processes involve the same basic steps – developing, bleaching and fixing (often the last two are combined in a single bleach-fix bath) – each type of film needs its own special process. So make sure you buy the right chemicals for your film.

1205 Storage
Colour process chemicals do not keep well. If you have to leave any part-used, make sure they are kept in temperatures above 61°F (16°C).

1206 Precision
For high-quality results, the temperatures of the process chemicals must be precisely controlled – the temperature of the first developer must be accurate to within 0.5°F (0.25°C) every time.

1207 Thermometer
For the accurate temperature measurement you need for colour processing, a mercury thermometer is essential. For complete accuracy, buy a high-quality thermometer and use it to calibrate a cheaper mercury thermometer which you can use for routine processing. To calibrate the cheaper thermometer, take readings from both thermometers as you warm up a water bath gradually and plot

the results on a graph. You can then read off the necessary adjustment to be made whenever you use the cheaper thermometer.

1208 Water bath
To ensure all colour chemicals are at the right temperature, stand their containers in a bath of water warmed to the right temperature. To keep the water bath at the right temperature, use a thermostatically controlled heating element or keep topping up the bath with warm water – watching the temperature and stirring all the while. See 1209.

1209 Dishwarmers
If you do plenty of colour work, it may be worth buying a dishwarmer to ensure the correct temperatures are maintained at all times. See 1208.

1210 Warm tanks
With some colour processes, precise developer temperature is so important that after loading the film into the tank (in complete darkness) you must prewarm both film and tank by pouring in water at the process temperature.

1211 Temperature checks
Always check developer temperature before pouring it into the tank. Check again after the first few minutes' development. If there is any sign of a substantial drop in temperature, add warm water to the water bath (**1208**) to bring the developer up to the required temperature.

1212 Air bubbles

Just as with b/w film, it is important to tap the developing tank firmly on the bench to free air bubbles that may be trapped on the film after pouring in developer.

1213 Consistent agitation

Consistent results with colour film processing depend, even more than with b/w, on always agitating the tank consistently. See 1143.

1214 Early pouring

Accurate development timing is so crucial with colour film that you must allow for the time solution takes to drain from the tank. Find out how long your tank takes to drain and, when developing, start emptying the tank this long before development time expires.

1215 Light-tight

Colour film is even more sensitive to stray light than b/w, so check your darkroom carefully for light leaks before you attempt to process colour film (see 1072). If you have any doubts whatsoever, load the film into the tank in a changing bag even in the darkroom.

1216 Processing slide film

If you can process colour negative film successfully, try your hand with colour slides. The two basic processes, E6 and P41, were invented by Kodak and Agfa respectively, but many other companies make processing kits.

1217 E6 processing

If you do much E6 processing (1216), consider buying a processing machine for easy temperature control.

1218 P41 processing

Use a clear plastic spiral when processing by the P41 method (1216) to ensure the film is evenly fogged (as the process requires) when you expose it to light after the reversal bath. (E6 is chemically fogged.) Otherwise, carefully unspool the film from the spiral and place it in a bowl of water at the process temperature. Then flash the film for a minute each side with a 150W bulb 12in (30cm) away.

1219 Weird colour

For weird colours, process E6-type slide film (see 1055, 1216) in colour negative chemicals.

1220 Push-processing

You can extend development time with colour slide film to gain film speed just as you can with b/w. With E6 (1213) an extra 2 mins development makes the film one stop faster; 6 mins makes it two stops faster.

1221 Copy slides

When processing copy colour slides, cut development time by $\frac{1}{3}$ to reduce contrast.

COLOUR PRINTING

1228
Never mix chemicals anywhere they might come into contact with food – many colour chemicals are extremely poisonous.

1229
Beware of getting colour printing chemicals on your hands. Rinse any splashes off immediately. Even those chemicals that are not dangerous can ruin any materials they touch.

1230
Don't use exposures shorter than 10 secs – it is impossible to time them accurately without a high-quality timer, and dodging and burning-in (1184–1188) are out of the question.

1231 Filter facilities
You can make colour prints with any enlarger, but it is much easier if you have one with a filter drawer or, better still, a dial-in colour head.

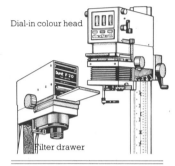

Dial-in colour head

Filter drawer

1232 Light-tight
Check the light-tightness of your darkroom in the way described in 1072 – colour paper is even more sensitive to stray light than b/w paper.

1233 Safelight
For colour negative paper (giving prints from negatives) you need a dim, dark amber or brown safelight. Colour reversal papers (giving prints from slides) must be handled in total darkness.

1234 The right paper
Choose paper and process to suit the film. With colour negatives, there are two basic types: type A (Kodak) and type B (Agfa). For Kodak films, use type A papers; for Agfa and most other films use type B. You can use the Cibachrome process to make prints from any slide films, but the Ektachrome 14RC process may be better with Ektachrome slides.

1235 Emulsion side
You can identify the dark brown emulsion side of Cibachrome by stroking a tiny corner with a finger nail – the non-emulsion side is slightly rougher and rustles. With Ektachrome 14RC paper, the emulsion side will feel slightly tacky if you moisten your finger and pinch a corner.

1236 Exposure tests
Before you attempt any filtration make a test strip just as for b/w printing (see 1179–1180) to establish the correct exposure. This test is often called a 'zero print' because zero filtration is used. If you are processing in a drum (see 1264) use a whole sheet of paper to ensure even processing.

1237 Exposure times
All colour papers but Cibachrome are much more sensitive than b/w papers, so halve the times you would use for exposure tests for b/w (see 1179–1180). See also 1236.

1238 Fine tuning
Precise exposure is essential with colour prints, so take the best exposure given by the zero print and make a second test, using a narrow range of times either side.

1239 Reversal prints
Remember, when printing from slides, that unlike b/w and colour negatives, they need more exposure for a lighter print and less exposure for a darker print. Check the print against the original slide to see if the exposure is correct.

1240 Filtration

Whenever you make a print from a colour negative, you must filter the enlarger light to correct for the amber colour of the film. Filtration is also needed to correct for any additional colour casts when printing from slides or negatives.

1241 Reference print

Before making your first print from a colour negative, have a large quality print made professionally from a well-exposed negative with a wide range of colours, preferably including skin tones. This will act as a reference for your first filtration experiments.

1242 Reference slide

The big advantage of printing from slides is that you can compare the colour in the print with the original slide directly. This makes gauging filtration quite simple. Examine them by daylight whenever possible, holding the slide against a sheet of white paper.

1243 Standard negative

For your first print, enlarge the same negative that was used for the reference print (1241). Once you have established the correct filtration for this (1245–1247) you can use it as a standard for all future negatives shot on the same film. See 1250.

1244 New paper batch

Every new batch of colour paper manufactured has a different colour balance and sensitivity, but there is no need to make a new standard (1243) for each new batch. Simply look at the filter balance and exposure factor marked on the packet, compare it with the figures for the previous batch and adjust accordingly

1245 Quadrant test

To establish the correct filtration, make a quadrant test. This is similar to a b/w test strip (1179–1180), except that you divide the picture into quarters rather than vertical strips, and instead of different exposure times you give each quarter different filtration.

1246 First tests

You may need to conduct a number of quadrant tests (1245) simply to establish the colour of the cast that needs correcting. Start with combinations of Yellow (Y) and Magenta (M) filters with colour negatives to correct the basic amber cast.

1247 Second tests

Once you have established the colour of the cast (1245–1246), you need to establish its density – that is, how strong the filters need to be to correct it.

1248 Filter factors

Printing filters cut down light so you must adjust exposure.

1249

Beware when using a colour analyser to establish filtration requirements – it is not infallible. Ask yourself if the picture has an unusually high proportion of one colour that may mislead the analyser. If the picture shows someone wearing a plain red dress against a crimson background, the analyser will assume that the picture has a red or magenta cast and indicate the necessary correction.

1250

Don't try to judge the colour or density of a test print (1243, 1245–1247) until it is dry. See also 1253.

1251
Never use yellow, magenta and cyan filters in combination – two colours are ALWAYS the most you need. If you use three, one of them will inevitably cancel out the effects of the others. If your tests indicate a filtration of Y25, M60 and C15, for example, take out the C15 and subtract 15 from the value of each of the other two, leaving you with Y10 M45. The only effect the C15 has is to increase the exposure needed. See **1252**, **1253**.

1252
Don't add filters to achieve the right filtration if you can possibly help it. Rather than adding a magenta, for instance, take away yellow and cyan instead. See **1251**.

1253
Never judge filtration (**1245–1247**, **1251–1252**) by safelight: it is very misleading. Take the print out into the daylight – or at least use normal 'white' artificial light. See also **1250**.

1254 Low values
Try to keep your experimental filter corrections to low values (05 and 10). Only use stronger filters if you are sure they are necessary.

1255 Filter aids
If you find it difficult to identify the colour of a cast, buy a filter mosaic. This consists of two 'cubes' of filters which you lay over colour paper and expose to an out-of-focus image of the negative. The square that gives a neutral grey image is the correctly filtered square.

1256 What colour?
With colour negative printing, colour casts are removed by increasing the strength of the filtration of the same colour. So a yellow cast is reduced by using stronger yellow filtration. With colour slide prints, on the other hand, the opposite is true. A yellow cast is reduced by reducing the yellow filtration. See also **1255**.

1257 Complementary
Most colour printing processes use filters in yellow, magenta and cyan. These are complementary colours, halfway between the primary colours (red, blue, and green) on the colour wheel. To achieve a primary colour, simply combine the two complementaries on either side.

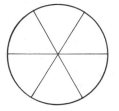

1258 Making notes
Always write down the filtration (**1245–1247**) at every stage to make sure you improve the filtration with every test. Then write the correct exposure and filtration on the back of every finished print so that if you ever want to make copies, you can use the same values again.

1259 New negatives
There is no need to go through a full series of tests with every new negative. Simply compare the zero print (**1236**) with that for the standard negative and estimate the correction needed.

1260 Fading filters
Colour filters fade with time, so check yours against new ones every couple of years.

1261 Lamp check
Enlarger lamps change in brightness and colour as they age, so keep a regular check with your standard negative or slide (**1243**) and correct as necessary when printing.

1262 Variable voltage
The mains voltage supply to your enlarger can vary. It is usually higher at night and lower at peak demand times. This can have a significant effect on colour balance. Make checks with your standard negative or slide and fit a voltage stabilizer if there are severe fluctuations.

1263 Ektachrome paper
Unlike Cibachrome, you must process Ektachrome immediately after exposure.

1264 Processing drum
By far the simplest way to process colour prints is in a print processing drum. This is quite like a film developing tank, only it is held horizontally during processing rather than vertically. Drums only take a limited range of paper sizes and can only be used for one print at a time, but they make up for this in terms of convenience and security – once the print is in the tank, you can safely switch on white light. See also **1265**.

1265 Rapid printing
If you want to make a large number of prints in a hurry, dish processing is better than drum processing (**1264**). But be careful not to switch on the light during processing, or allow to much carry-over of developer to the bleach-fix bath.

1266 Continuous feed
If you have money to spare and are tired of the effort of processing manually, your problems will be solved by a continuous feed processor such as the Durst. You simply feed the print in one end – the processor does the rest.

1267 Drum technique
By taping several small pieces of colour printing paper back to back, you can 'bulk' process in a print processing drum with no danger of paper overlap.

1268 Drain time
As with colour films, you must allow time for the print processing drum to drain when timing development. See **1214**.

1269 Dry run
Always squeegee colour prints before hanging them up to dry.

1270 Rapid dry
To dry colour test strips quickly (see **1250**), wipe them down with tissues and hold them in front of a fan heater.

1271 Streaks
If your colour prints are streaky or covered in marks, it is probably due to poor agitation. If no amount of agitation seems to cure the streaks, try using a c22-type stop bath for one minute followed by a one-minute wash then normal bleach-fixing

1272 Large slides
To make large slides from colour negatives, print on to Kodak Vericolor print film 4111 or Vericolor slide film 5072 and process as prints. To make large slides from slides, make a negative copy first.

1273 Quick and easy
If you want a quick, foolproof, no-fuss method of colour printing, try the Kodak Ektaflex or Agfachrome-Speed systems. Both these systems need only a single processing solution and give high-quality results from both slides and negatives. But with Ektaflex you need a print-maker that costs as much as a simple enlarger.

1274
Don't risk wasting expensive colour printing paper by using exhausted chemicals. Most colour print processes are 'one shot' – that is, they are to be used once, then discarded.

1275
Don't forget to dry a print processing drum before you put the print in.

1276
Don't worry too much about maintaining the temperature with a quick colour printing process if using a drum: quick colour processes are so quick that the temperature loss is insignificant. Start with the drum a few degrees above the recommended temperature. By the end of the process, the temperature may have dropped a little, but the average should be near enough.

1277
Don't try to dish process colour prints without some means of controlling the temperature accurately. With large, open surfaces, heat is lost quickly. Use a thermostatically controlled dish warmer.

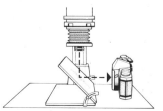

1278
Don't allow any stray light into the room when making duplicate slides by shooting the screen as in **1283**. Shield the light spilling from the projector lamp housing, but do not leave a cover in place long enough for the lamp to overheat.

1279
Never look into the viewfinder with the camera lens at full aperture if shooting directly into a projector for slide-copying (**1284**). The bright light can damage the eyes. To frame up, stop down to the minimum aperture (**170**).

1280
Watch for specks of dust on slides to be duplicated. Clean them off thoroughly with a blower brush or jet from an aerosol cleaner.

1281
Be sure to get slides for duplicating the right way round before shooting. In a projector or enlarger (**1283, 1285**) the non-emulsion side (**1415**) must face the light source. In a barrel copier (**1287**) the non-emulsion side faces 'into' the camera.

1282 Irreplaceable slides
If you have valuable or ir-replaceable slides, why not make copies ('dupes') of them and put the originals safely away?

1283 Projection copy
If you possess a slide projector and a screen, the simplest way to make slide copies is to photograph the image on the screen. Load the camera with tungsten-balanced film: most projectors have tungsten halogen bulbs. And for quality, use the minimum possible enlargement.

1284 Extension tubes
If you have a set of extension tubes, you can get better quality dupes than from shooting a slide screen if you remove the lens from a slide projector and shoot directly into the gate of the projector.

1285 Enlarger copies
Anyone who owns an enlarger has the facilities to make really high-quality dupes at his disposal. All you need is a front-silvered mirror to turn the projected image through 90° into the camera (with the camera lens removed). You can buy special mirrors specifically for this purpose complete with a bracket for holding the camera.

1286
If the head of your enlarger turns to project an image on to a wall, you do not even need a front-silvered mirror (**1285**). Simply put the camera on a tripod and project the image into the camera.

1287 Barrel copier
If you want to make plenty of copies simply for reference, buy a cheap barrel copier. It contains its own close-up lens. Follow the maker's instructions, focusing carefully against a bright light; see also **1288**.

1288 Flash dupes
The best source of illumination for a barrel copier (**1287**) is an electronic flashgun fired by a remote control cable. The distance from the gun to the slide determines exposure. Make a series of test exposures at distances of about 6in (15cm), 14in (35cm), 25in (63cm) and 54in (137cm).

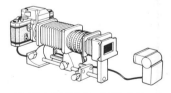

1289 Filters
Experiment with filters to correct colour when copying.

1290 Contrast control
If you find contrast in your dupes too high, remove the slide after normal exposure and without winding on (see Assignment **8**) expose again with the lens at f22.

1291 Prognosis
All prints fade eventually, but you can make them last longer than otherwise by processing with care. See 1292–1306.

1292 Fixing
If you want prints to last, fix them in two stages, transferring the prints from one fresh batch of fixer to another. Make sure the temperature of the fixer stays between 64°F (18°C) and 75°F (24°C). To make fixing absolutely foolproof, use old-fashioned hypo rather than modern, high-speed fixer.

1293 Hypo clearance
To be absolutely sure that all traces of fixer are removed, rinse the print in Kodak hypo clearing agent (10% sodium carbonate solution) before the wash commences.

1294 Washing
Thorough washing is as important for print permanence as fixing. You can test the efficiency of your wash by adding a little household dye to the water – it should vanish within five minutes.

1295 Test for fixer
After washing, test for residual traces of fixer by putting a drop of silver nitrate solution on the edge of the print, in an area that is to be trimmed off. If a brown or black stain appears, there are still traces of fixer and the print must be washed again thoroughly. If this happens persistently, soak for one minute in 1.8 pints (1 litre) of water with $\frac{1}{3}$ fl oz (10ml) of ammonia and $\frac{1}{3}$ fl oz (10 ml) hydrogen peroxide before

washing, and try to improve your washing technique.

1296 Cascades
The best way to wash prints is in a cascade system. Arrange dishes in a series of steps beneath the tap (faucet), so that water runs from a high-level dish into a succession of lower dishes. Start washing the print in the lowest dish and then move it up in stages to the top dish where the water is purest.

1297 Wetting agent
For perfect drying, rinse prints in a solution of wetting agent made up with distilled water, ten times more dilute than recommended by the makers.

1298 Drying prints
The simplest way to dry prints is to hang them on a line in pairs, back-to-back, using plastic clothes pegs at all four corners. See also 1299.

1299
If you don't have room for a line (1298) dry the prints face down on fibreglass screens

1300
Don't let prints sit in the fixer – keep them on the move.

1301
Don't use resin-coated (RC) paper – it tends to have a shorter life (20 years or so) than fibre-based paper.

1302
Avoid fixing a print more than necessary – no amount of washing can remove the fixer from an over-fixed print.

1303
Never allow traces of chemicals to build up on dishes and surfaces in the darkroom. See 1095.

1304
Don't use print flattening solutions – they attract moisture and will soon spoil the prints. If your prints curl, stack them up and compress them with heavy books for a few days.

1305
Don't store prints in a wooden cupboard or box – some woods give off gases that can harm photo papers. Stove enamelled steel cabinets are best.

SPECIAL EFFECTS

1306
Don't overdo special effects – they can soon become very tedious.

1307
Don't forget to cover the enlarger baseboard with absorbent material when taking the wet print from the developer for the fogging exposure in solarization (1309).

1308
Don't expect to be able to repeat your results if you solarize a print (1309). The technique is notoriously unpredictable. If you want to make copies, solarize the negative instead. You can do this by exposing the film to white light half-way through development, but the best way is to make a copy of the negative on Kodak Fine Grain Positive type 5302 film, which can be handled in normal darkroom safelighting. Then use the resulting positive to make another negative on 5302 – you can solarize this negative in exactly the same way as a b/w print.

1309 Solarized prints
If you want a print that is just a little out of the ordinary, you can 'solarize' it and make it glow like white-hot metal. All you have to do is 'fog' it (expose it to white light) half-way through development. Simply expose a normal print from your chosen negative and put it in a light-tight container. Remove the negative and expose a test strip (see 1179) to find the correct fogging exposure – neutral grey with b/w. Then develop the print for half the time; place it on the enlarger baseboard (covered in plastic and absorbent material); make the fogging exposure; and develop normally. See also 1310–1311; 1307–1308.

1310 Old developer
To enhance the solarized effect, use partially exhausted developer left out overnight.

1311 Colour effects
Solarizing colour prints can be even more unpredictable than with b/w. For a range of weird effects, you can make the fogging exposure through different-coloured filters.

1312 Old masters
For a striking 'painted' effect, expose a print as normal and then brush strong developer solution on selected areas of the print and develop normally. Use the brush to emphasize certain parts of the picture.

1313 Agfa contour
For an effect similar to solarization (1309), but more predictable, use Agfa contour paper.

1314 Distortion
Stretch some parts of a print and compress others by curving or tilting the paper under the enlarger.

1315 Smear tactics
To get shadows diffusing into highlights of a print, lay a sheet of glass smeared with petroleum jelly over the print for half the exposure time. The diffusion pattern depends on how the jelly is smeared.

1316 Photograms
By laying all kinds of objects on printing paper and exposing it to white light, you can make outline images (photograms) without even loading a camera. Try objects such as leaves, flowers, or blocks of ice.

1317 Texture
To give your pictures all kinds of interesting textures, print through a texture screen. You can buy them ready-made, but far better make your own by photographing a suitable surface, such as a fine cloth or piece of stonework, then sandwiching this with the negative in the enlarger. Underexpose the texture shot slightly to keep the negative thin. Another way of achieving texture is to lay fine muslin over the paper for part of the exposure.

STORAGE AND PRESENTATION

Preserving, and enjoying the results

1318
Don't store negatives in materials which are not designed for the job. Some plastics and papers give off gases that will fade the image.

1319
Don't cut off waste film at the end of a strip. An inch or two of spare makes handling easier and helps keep the negative flat in the enlarger.

1320
Don't store negatives rolled up. It always leads to scratching and the film will be curly – hard to keep flat.

1321 Remember
Adequate fixing, washing and drying is vital if negatives are not to deteriorate. Poor fixing causes fogging, poor washing local fading. Dampness encourages mould, as well as making the negatives stick to the file sheet and each other. Extremely thorough fixing and washing are needed to make negatives last well.

1322 Best filing system
Sheets that hold seven strips of six 35mm negatives allow a whole film to be kept in order in one file. Similar sheets with larger pockets are available for rollfilm.

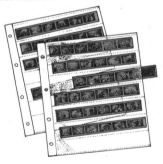

1323 Transparent sheets
Consider transparent plastic file sheets if you make repeated sets of contact prints of each film. They save time and handling damage because the contacts can be printed without removing the negatives. Use a Chinagraph (grease pencil) or washable felt-tip pen to write details on the sheet; they'll print on the contact sheet, too. This system has a drawback: contacts of a whole 35mm film will not fit on to a 10 × 8in sheet of printing paper.

1324 Negative albums
Purpose-made negative albums with four rings hold file sheets most securely.

1325 Cool and dry
For negatives, relative humidity should not exceed 60 per cent. The temperature should be below 60°F (15°C). Don't store negatives where these conditions change often or rapidly. See 1327.

1326 Colour care
Colour negatives need the same storage control as black and white (see 1325, 1327), but a higher degree of care. They must be stored in the dark. Bad storage makes colour dyes fade at different rates, resulting in colour balance shift.

1327 Fumes
Store negatives well away from rooms heated by gas or coal fires, raw wood or other sources of fumes. See 1325.

1328 Dodge
If a particular negative needs a specially shaped dodge or card mask for printing, store it with the negative's file.

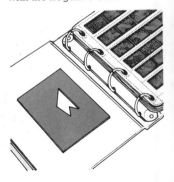

1329 Reference
The only truly efficient method of retrieving specific negatives from a filing system (1322, 1324) is a numbering system. Every album should be numbered, as should every negative file sheet. Frames are of course numbered already by the manufacturer. Using this system, the 10th frame of the 75th sheet of the third album would be 3/75/10.

1330 File box
Use file cards in a box numbered to correspond with the negative sheets for recording details of exposure, processing and any special treatment. Equally, enter details about the subject, occasion, plus printing notes for future reference.

1331 Filing by subject
An alternative way of storing negatives is to have a separate album for each subject, for example vacations, friends, hobbies. If you take a lot of pictures and in due course the files become too full, break them down into sub-groups – vacations can be broken down into countries, and so on.

1332 Away from home
If your negatives are stored by someone else, write your name and file reference numbers (1329) in the margin of each storage sheet (1322).

1333
Don't store more than one negative strip in the same bag, or the same pocket of a file sheet: they are likely to stick together.

1334
Don't cut negatives into short strips or single frames. Lengths of six frames are easiest to handle.

1335
Don't write on storage bags or sheets when the negatives are inside.

1336
Don't store negatives without first removing fingerprints: these will eat into the emulsion eventually.

STORING PRINTS

1337
Don't store prints where they may get damp. The images will deteriorate.

1338
Don't store prints where there are frequent temperature changes, such as lofts or attics.

1339
Don't store prints in sealed boxes or in tins where there is no airflow to combat dampness – but see 1352. Avoid storing them in wooden boxes or cupboards – see 1305.

1340
Avoid using scissors for trimming prints. Unless the print is tiny, and you make each trim in just one cut, it is hard to achieve a neat,* straight edge with scissors. Use a guillotine or paper cutter, and beware of blunt ones. Or, use a scalpel – craft knife – and metal straightedge. Scalpel blades and craft knives are available form artists' suppliers.

1341 Albums
If you store your prints in albums, use ones with large pages: they give much more scope for practical and imaginative arrangements.

1342 Small prints
These are usually best kept in an album; they are a nuisance to search out in a box or filing cabinet storage system.

1343 Variety
Create an interesting and attractive-looking album by varying the appearance of pages with different print sizes. One small print of an outstanding picture could carry a whole page; one big print may gain by being surrounded with smaller ones.

1344 Trimmer
Is your guillotine (paper cutter) not as sharp as you would wish? If it's the type with a swinging blade, and you must use it before it is re-sharpened, give the blade a little extra bite by pressing it in to the left, hard against the base plate cutting edge as you slice the prints.

1345 Cut-outs
Pictures cluttered up with unnecessary detail are all too common, as are pictures with just one interesting element, surrounded by unnecessary detail, unattractive background, overexposed sky and so on. Why not cut out the best part of the print (throw away the rest) and stick that in your album? You can combine cutouts with rectangular prints, gaining impact and variety; or you can run the occasional page of nothing but cut-outs. The many different shapes in themselves add an extra dimension to an album.

1346 Expansion
Obviously, expanding albums are practical; and the most practical expanding album is the type with covers and leaves held together by long screws. The covers always lie flat, however many new leaves you add; longer screws can be bought when the existing ones cannot carry any more leaves.

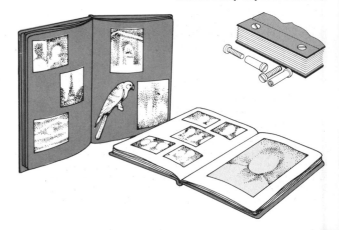

1347 Album types
Gluing prints into albums is time-consuming and surprisingly hard to do well (see 1349), which accounts for the popularity of 'peel apart' photo albums, in which the prints are sandwiched into position under a layer of transparent acetate. Remember, however, that static electricity builds up on the acetate, and it can be easy to sandwich in dirty specks as well as your prints. Work in dust-free conditions, and have an anti-static cloth by you.

1348 Back-to-back
Compact and convenient (no glue, no problems with static) storage for up to 100 $3\frac{1}{2} \times 5\frac{1}{2}$in (9cm × 14cm) prints is the simple back-to-back album. Prints just slide in and out of the sleeves.

1349 Adhesives
Spray adhesives are convenient, giving even, flat attachment, and allowing repositioning. However, some spray adhesives have been suspected as health hazards; but 3M, manufacturers of Spraymount, state no cancer-causing constituents are present in

it. If gluing prints conventionally, use light paper paste, single dabs at corners. Glue soaks through paper, making it damp; interleave with blotting paper.

1350 Box storage
Empty photographic paper boxes make useful storage for larger prints. Write details on edge of box, and see 1356–1358.

1351 Writing on prints
Use the softest grade of pencil for writing on the back of fibre-based prints, and likewise for resin-coated papers. Don't press hard - it can show through at the front side. Use a spirit-based felt-tip pen to write on the front of a print - the ink dries fast

1352 Hot, damp climates
Mould and fungus ruin pictures quickly. If the climate is rainy-tropical, store prints in sealed tins with a small cloth bag containing silica gel (obtainable from chemists and drugstores). This absorbs moisture. Every two months, bake the silica gel in a moderate oven to drive out water, then reuse it.

1353 Bulk storage
For large numbers of large prints, the best solution is an office filing cabinet with suspension files.

1354 Filing
File by subject. If a photo fits more than one category, file under the most obvious and, under the others, insert cards with details of the 'master'.

1355
Check prints are dry before storing them in containers. They will stick together if damp, and damage other prints.

1356
Don't put prints inside the black plastic bags which printing papers are packed in. It is extremely efficient at sealing in damp.

1357
Avoid, if possible, stacking print storage boxes flat. Contact pressure can make prints stick together. Stand the boxes upright instead.

1358
Avoid storing prints in more than two or, at the most, three different sizes of box. Many box sizes are hard to store efficiently.

1359
Ensure the nozzle of a spray mounting can is clean before using, otherwise small bumps caused by hard blobs may develop on the mounted print surface. After use, hold the can upside down and give a short squirt to clear the jet.

DISPLAYING PRINTS

1360
Don't hang colour prints in direct sunlight. It has a bleaching effect, and colours fade at different rates.

1361
Don't ignore the effect different viewing lights have on the appearance of photographs. Colour contrast and saturation will in particular be very different in daylight and fluorescent light. Experiment before making a final choice.

1362
Never, when dry mounting (1364) with a domestic iron, apply full heat to the print without first experimenting on a corner of the print. The right heat for efficient dry mounting with an iron is found by trial and error, and governed by variable factors such as the power of the iron and thickness of the photo paper. Excessive heat will spoil prints.

1363 Quick mounts
Simple but fast and inexpensive mounts for prints are made by cutting a sheet of hardboard or plywood to the same size as the print and sticking print to hardboard with double-sided tape. Fix the tape to the hardboard first, then stand print and board up on edge so they are touching at the bottom. Then bring them together. This gives accurate attachment first time.

1364 Dry mounting
The most permanent, flat and professional mounting method is to use dry-mounting tissue, readily available from photo dealers. The simplest and most foolproof way of using it is in a purpose-designed dry mounting press. But these are expensive, and it is often difficult to get access to one unless perhaps by membership of a photo club. However, you can dry mount with a domestic iron. Trim the tissue exactly to the size of the print. Tack it to the back of the print, gently, with the tip of a medium-hot iron. Position the print on the mounting card, face up. Cover with a sheet of thick smooth-quality paper. Having tested on a corner (see 1362), apply the iron to the covering sheet, pressing hard and keeping it moving. Attachment takes 20–30 seconds.

1365 Clip mounts
Sandwich prints between hardboard and glass and clamp together with chrome clips. These are available from photo dealers or artists' suppliers.

1366 Tape mounts
As an alternative to clips (1365), use heavy-duty adhesive tape. Black and white prints look good with chrome-coloured or black tape. With colour prints, choose a colour that is complementary to the main colour in the photo.

1367 Glass
If reflections in the glass of a frame spoil the look of a print, buy non-reflective glass.

Clips   Tape   Metal   Wood

1368
Ordinary window glass often has bubbles and other flaws that detract from the appearance of a framed print. For a better result, use special selected-quality glass.

1369 Card mounts
Make small prints look impressive by mounting them on a large piece of card.

1370 Coloured mounts

Prints gain impact, even look different, if mounted on appropriately coloured board. Find the right colour by taking the print to the shop where you buy the board and holding the print against various colours before making the selection.

1371 For landscapes

Landscapes gain an impression of depth if mounted on a black card with a fine white line around the edge of the image. The easy way to achieve the white line is to have the print made with a white border, then trim it down to a millimetre or so all round with a scalpel and straightedge.

1372 Light edges

If there are areas of light tone round the edges of a print, try drawing a fine black line round the image. Not only will the image seem to spring out from the paper, it will seem sharper.

1373 Sets

Groups of pictures can add to each other's impact. So try making up sets of prints of related subjects and display them in similar mounts in matching colours. See 1374–1375.

1374

If you are mounting a set of prints in one large frame (1373), attempt to arrange them in appropriate patterns. Static images usually work best in a symmetrical pattern. Strong, dynamic images can be eye-catching in a diagonal line.

1375

Tell the story of a trip or special occasion by choosing between four and eight of the best pictures you took and mounting them in sequence.

1376 Shapes

Prints do not have to be rectangular. Try cutting a circular or diamond shape out of a photo for a change.

1377

Look at the composition of a photograph and cut the picture to a shape that suits it.

1378

Don't overdo it – particularly if you are displaying prints as suggested in 1373–1375. Simple ideas usually work better than complicated ones. A small number of good pictures look better than plenty of nearly good ones.

DISPLAYING PRINTS

1379
Don't start from the top when making a mobile (1382). The secret of making a mobile that balances well is to start with the bottom pieces and work upwards, ensuring each level balances before moving to the next.

1380 Paperweights
Try making prints into paperweights – one of the most attractive and practical of the unconventional methods of print display. They have to be cast in clear acrylic resin (Lucite) – the type commonly used by sculptors. Use a ready-made mould, or one made by yourself from special rubber compound. Resin, moulds and rubber compound are available from serious art suppliers. Use a small print, colour or black and white, and make sure the surface is clean and grease-free. Pour a little resin into the mould, and when it has set, place the print face-down on a thin layer of fresh resin. Press gently into place to remove air bubbles, then pour more resin on top. When it has set, any small marks can be removed with metal polish.

1381 Photocloths
Professional photo suppliers can supply or obtain cloth coated with photographic emulsion for black and white prints. Print directly on to this, developing in the normal way, to create photographic table mats, or flags. See also 1383.

1382 Mobile
Cut up spare colour prints and make them into a mobile. Use thin wire for the cross-pieces and cotton or nylon thread for hanging the components. Choose colourful images, especially if constructing the mobile for a baby. See 1379.

1383 Liquid emulsion
Photographic emulsion is available from professional photo suppliers in liquid form. Try painting it on to an attractively grained, preferably pale wooden surface. Make the print in the usual way. The result will show the texture and grain of the wood. Screw eyelets into the back, attach picture wire and hang without framing or glass to get the best effect. See also 1381.

1384
Even more unusual than coating liquid photographic emulsion on wood (1383) is to use it on a three-dimensional object such as an egg or glass jug. Printing on the curved suface gives a strikingly distorted image. Experiment, and remove failures (if dried-on) by wiping with household bleach and scraping.

1385 Keyring
Small prints or transparencies can be clipped into clear plastic mounts that attach to keyrings – useful stocking fillers.

1386 Wanted
Make 'Wanted for . . .' posters as presents for children by blowing up a suitable portrait with a wide margin at the top. Add the lettering by means of an instant lettering system, choosing an appropriate Wild West style of typeface, for example Broadway or Rockwell Extra Bold.

1387 Sheet film
Print negatives on to sheet film (1272) ('ordinary' and ortho types can be used under a safelight) to make a large-size transparency that can be glued or taped to a window pane. Process with print developer. Sandwich a sheet of tracing paper, or opal photo film, between the transparency and the glass to add extra body to the light parts of the image. Expect colours to face; slow this process by mounting the assembly on a window that receives a minimum of sunlight, and treat with an ultraviolet spray.

1388 Photo lampshade
Strip the cover from an old lampshade and replace it with tracing paper or opal photo film. Stick prints or transparencies to it with transparent tape and create an interesting display. Prints on resin-coated paper are especially suitable: it is possible to separate the image-bearing surface of the paper from the rest by carefully parting the natural layers of

the paper at one edge and slowly peeling it away. The resulting tissue-thin photo will light up brightly. See 1392.

1389 Mural
Really big enlargements have an impact all their own – provided the quality of the image can stand up to it. Kodak make rolls of photographic paper up to 40in (102cm) wide. Alternatively, join several smaller pieces and disguise the joints by retouching. However, making prints much larger than your usual maximum size can be more trouble than it is worth (you have to put plastic on the darkroom floor and sponge on the developer). Find out what a professional laboratory would charge. Convert an outsize print into a mural by mounting it directly to a wall with wallpaper adhesive, or attaching it to board. Use coarse-quality, fibre-based paper.

1390 Collage
Create an exhibition of favourite family photos by mounting cork sheeting or tiles over a generous area of kitchen wall. Pins with brightly coloured plastic heads are convenient for attaching the prints, and they look pretty. Be selective; change the prints regularly.

1391
Don't laminate a mural unless you are especially concerned to preserve it. Any laminating material – including adhesive film, glass and Perspex (Plexiglas) – makes a print highly reflective. Before it is hung in position, it is almost impossible to judge whether there will be a problem with reflection. Non-reflective glass will significantly reduce contrast and therefore the impact of a big print. Laminating film is in addition only available up to a certain maximum size: you may well be unable to cover the print in a single sheet.

1392
Watch closely for signs of warping when first trying out a slide display mounted on a lampshade as in 1388. Change to a less powerful bulb at the first sign of buckling. To allow the transparencies slight room for movement, don't fix them tightly on all four sides.

1393
Don't show work that is not your absolute best. A few first-class photographs give a better impression than the same pictures with some mediocre ones thrown in too.

1394
Take care when developing a set of prints for display purposes. Ensure they have perfect surfaces; use fresh developer and make doubly sure each is processed at the same temperature and for the same length of time. Variation can cause slight but disturbing changes in colour.

1395 Remember
If you want to have your work published, or simply display it to discerning people – privately, or in exhibitions – it pays to spend extra time on presentation. Picture editors and art directors see photographs from top professionals day in, day out. Work does not always have to be world-shattering, but it does have to be clean and well presented if it is to get a second look.

1396
Before you meet a picture editor or art director, be familiar with the work he or she uses. Is your work really suitable for his/her needs?

1397 The portfolio
If you have had work published, include some of the best in the portfolio, but see 1393. This way you will be viewed professionally.

1398 Monochrome prints
Black and white prints should be on a top-quality fibre-based paper such as Ilford Galerie.

1399 Colour prints
If you are showing colour prints made from slides, have them printed on Cibachrome rather than direct reversal paper. The colour and saturation of Cibachrome is superior.

1400 Transparencies
Colour slides look most impressive mounted in black card mounts available from professional photo suppliers. They have apertures cut to take up tp 20 35mm slides.

1401 Mounting
Use quality dry mounting tissue for mounting prints on board – not adhesive. It gives a flatter, more professional finish; but see 1364.

1402 Flat
It is surprising how much even unmounted prints are improved by flattening in a dry mounting press.

1403 Lamination
If prints are to be frequently handled, they will soon become dog-eared and tatty. The solution is to have them laminated – sealed between two layers of plastic film. This gives a permanent, hard-wearing finish which can be wiped clean with a damp cloth. Because the plastic is bonded to the paper, it does not spoil the image tones.

1404
Prevent laminated prints from scuffing against each other when stacked by sticking a felt-surfaced household laminate to the backs of prints.

1405 Windows
Really fine prints, particularly landscapes, look superb if they are mounted behind a 'window' cut in card. Cut the window just smaller than the image, choosing a suitable colour to offset a dominant colour or tone in the print. Fix the window over the mounted print with double-sided tape.

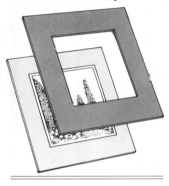

1406 Captions
Unless you have exceptionally neat handwriting, it is best to type captions on labels and attach them to prints, or to use an instant lettering system.

1407 Back-projectors
If you have a large number of slides to show, consider hiring a portable back-projection unit. These fit into a suit-case-sized carrier.

1408 Light boxes
If you happen to be involved in the selection of transparencies after a completed assignment, make sure that the light box is colour-corrected. If it is not, your slides may seem to have poor colour balance.

1409 Drying
Proper drying of prints is vital – see 1298. For an exceptionally fine, dull sheen, dry glossy papers face-down on muslin stretched over a frame.

1410 Calling card
An impressive but practical touch is to leave a photo-postcard after showing work. Professional labs will make them for you. Feature one of your best shots, and ask the lab to add your name, address and telephone number in a margin. Any description of your work should be extremely brief.

1411
Don't use water colours to spot prints. Only use purpose-made photographic dyes, which do not stand out. See also Assignment 10.

1412
Don't spoil fine work by presenting pictures in manufacturers' photo paper boxes. Top photo dealers sell a range of museum-quality storage boxes and portfolios.

1413
Avoid using clear plastic sleeves in portfolios. They reflect so much light that the blacks of prints inside can look grey.

1414
Take care to put slides in projectors or viewers the right way round. In a projector, the non-emulsion side should face the light source. In a viewer, it must be the side facing you. Kodachrome is customarily marked 'view from this side'. Other film types could present problems if you forget, or don't know which is the 'right' side: emulsion and non-emulsion sides look similar, though in fact the emulsion side is slightly duller than the other. See also **1422**.

1415
Don't use an old sheet as a slide projecting screen: it scatters light, making slides look dull. Draughts will distort the image.

1416
Don't use too many slides for a show; 100 is plenty for a sitting.

1417
Take care when sorting slides not to finger the image. Cotton gloves are the simple (and cheap) solution.

1418 Remember
Planning an outstanding slide show starts before you take the pictures. Think it through from beginning to end.

1419
Glass mounts give slides maximum protection. Buy mounts with anti-Newton's Rings (explained in **1014**) glass.

1420
When selecting slides for a show, eliminate poor exposures. Jumping from bright to dark images is disturbing. Copy underexposed images (**1282–1290**) giving extra exposure.

1421
If sorting slides on a light box, minimize eye strain by masking unused areas.

1422 Spotting
Mark the bottom left corner of each mount on the non-emulsion side (see **1414**) with a spot. Slides correctly inserted in the projector (i.e. upside down, with the non-emulsion side towards the light source) will show these spots at the top right-hand corner: easy to detect if wrongly inserted.

1423 Numbering
Once sorted, number the slides for a show: it saves time and trouble when loading.

1424 The room
It is worth lightproofing a room as best you can for a slide show. Effective black-out makes slides look brighter.

1425 Setting-up
Take trouble erecting projector and screen. If they aren't level and parallel in the vertical plane, the image will not be rectangular.

1426 Enlarging the image
If you lack the space to project a large image, use a mirror to lengthen the light path.

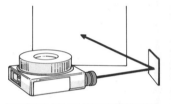

1427 Timing
Vary the time slides stay on the screen to give a pace that changes appropriately. Contemplative landscape shots can take up to 30 seconds on the screen. In general, four to 10 seconds is adequate.

1428 Titling
Write or draw on blank slides to create titles or illustrations.

1429
Make illustrated slide-titles by shooting a duplicate (**1282–1290**) of the chosen slide with part of the image masked. Using instant lettering, put down the title on coloured paper so that it fills the required area. Photograph this, and combine the two slides.

1430
Try photographing postcards or vacation brochures as introductory features for a show.

1431 Special mounts
Slide mounts are available in a wide number of special shapes. Make your own by cutting out black card and fixing it over the existing mount.

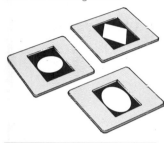

1432 Two projectors
To achieve a really slick show, use two projectors: you need never have a blank screen as the image changes. Alternate slides between the projectors. Keep the projector lenses close together by stacking units on top of each other.

1433 Instant mural
Some social occasions can be enhanced by a backdrop slide show. A rock concert scene, projected on to a convenient wall, could set the mood for a discotheque. Use a projector with an efficient cooling system.

1434 Sound
Even simple slide shows run more smoothly with background sound: play it at low volume.

1435
If you possess a stereo cassette player you can put the cues for slide changing on one track and the sound track on the other. Play the sound track

through one speaker and listen to the other track through headphones to hear the cues.

1436
An alternative way (see 1435) to cue your slide changes against a sound track is to write a script of the sound track. Mark changes in the margin.

1437 Positioning speakers
If your sound system has separate speakers, put them behind the screen for the best effect.

1438 Editing
Reel-to-reel tape recorders are best for editing sound, but you can transfer selected sections of one cassette to another by connecting the headphone output of one machine to the microphone input of another.

1439
For a really professional show, hire an auto-changing tape/slide synchronizer.

1440 Recording
If outdoors, cut a slot in a sponge and slip the microphone in to cut wind noise.

1441
Keep the microphone close to the person speaking to cut out background noise.

1442
When asking questions for your sound track interviews, avoid questions that can be answered 'yes' or 'no'. Ask open-ended questions.

1443
Take extra care with exposure of b/w slides; bracket (161) to ensure results.

1444
Don't use the automatic recording level control if your equipment also offers a manual setting. Automatic makes the background noise louder when the main sound stops.

1445
Don't wave recording equipment around when the tape is running: this can affect the speed of the motor, distorting sound.

1446
Don't record sound emitted by a loudspeaker through a microphone. The result is 'fuzzy'.

ACKNOWLEDGEMENTS

ARTWORK
All line drawings by **Tony Graham** except 1041, 1127, 1131, 1132, 1144, 1165, 1169, 1187, 1194, 1213 – **John Bishop;** 1080, 1101, 1102, 1111, 1117, 1322, 1328, 1330, 1346, 1348, 1363, 1367, 1395, 1405, 1407, 1408, 1426, 1431 – **Jim Robbins.**

PHOTOGRAPHS
Nick Scott: Contents 1, 2, 3, 8, 9, 10; section openers Technique, Subjects, Equipment, Processing and Darkroom; tips 214, 244, 247, 270, 290, 295, 305, 347, 366, 381, 385, 452, 459, 488, 528, 656, 665, 687, 718, 918, 1181, 1314, 1390, 1410. **MPA:** Contents 4, 5, 6; 220, 222, 233, 311, 431, 462, 479, 482, 549, 593, 595, 598, 602, 603, 611, 616, 643, 647, 657, 678, 688, 794, 1035. **Robert Harding Picture Library Ltd:** tips 314, 377, 506, 523, 532, 541, 577, 583, 675, 691, 692, Further Assignments. **Paddy Eckersley:** Assignments 7 and 9. **Monique Fey:** Assignment 3, tip 1061. **Michael Freeman:** Assignments 12 and 13. **Brian Griffin:** Assignments 7 and 16. **Gered Mankowitz;** tips 438, Assignment 16. **Eamonn McCabe;** tip 534, Assignment 5. **Chris Alan Wilton/Image Bank:** Contents 7, Assignment 8. **DA:** tips 627, 631, 633. **Nigel O'Gorman:** tips 737, 747. **Aerofilms:** tip 613. **Heather Angel:** Assignment 4. **James Barrow/Robert Harding Picture Library:** Assignment 6. **Roy Flooks:** Assignment 15. **Cliff Feulner/Image Bank:** Assignment 1. **David Hamilton/Image Bank:** Assignment 2. **Liz Hollingworth:** Assignment 11. **Lawrence Lawry:** Assignment 9. **Bill and Claire Leimbach:** Assignment 6. **Fiona Pragoff:** tip 576. **Mike Roles:** section opener Storage and Presentation. **Scottish Tourist Board:** tip 691. **Tim Shackleton:** tip 43. **Anthea Sieveking/Vision International:** Assignment 14. **Helena Zakrzewska-Rucinska** (photographs by Peter Mackertich): Assignment 10. Retouching by **Roy Flooks** throughout.

EDITORIAL/DESIGN
Editors: **John Farndon, Tim Shackleton;** designers: **Nigel O'Gorman, Paulene Faulks;** research: **Ivan Chilvers, Sally Walters;** editorial assistance: **Fred and Kathie Gill;** art editor: **Mel Petersen;** production: **Bull Publishing Consultants.**

Thanks also to Peter Southerst and Peter Lester.